IS YOUR CHURCH ON LIFE SUPPORT?

Rudy Hall

Remnant Publications, Coldwater, MI

Copyright © 2013 by
Remnant Publications

All Rights Reserved
Printed in the USA

Published by
Remnant Publications
649 East Chicago Road
Coldwater MI 49036
800-423-1319
www.remnantpublications.com

Unless otherwise noted, Scripture quotations are taken
from the New King James Version. Copyright © 1982 by
Thomas Nelson, Inc. Used by permission. All rights reserved.

Scripture quotations marked KJV are taken
from the Holy Bible, King James Version.

Copy Edited by Debi Tesser
Cover designed by David Berthiaume
Text designed by Greg Solie • Altamont Graphics

ISBN: 978-1-937718-73-2

Content

Introduction 5

Chapter 1   What Is Going on with That Little Church? 7

Chapter 2   Failure: The First Step to Success 11

Chapter 3   A Visit Causes Changes 21

Chapter 4   Been There, Done That 27

Chapter 5   A Time for Decision and Direction 33

Chapter 6   First Order of Business 39

Chapter 7   The Pastor Leaves, So What? 45

Chapter 8   The Missing Place 49

Chapter 9   The New Pastor Arrives 55

Chapter 10   Dealing with the Devil 61

Chapter 11   Time for a Rest 67

Chapter 12   Power of Choice 75

Chapter 13   Send Them Away! 83

Chapter 14   Six to Sixty 91

Introduction

When I was asked by a pastor to help revitalize a dying church, I took the challenge, but for some reason my efforts failed. Then just a few years later, I was asked to work with another church, which also had just a few members. After my first failing experience, I had no interest in jumping back into the water. However, the request was persistent. Eventually, and reluctantly, I said, "Yes." Amazingly, this time it was a great success. I had tried my best and put my heart and soul into each church. Why did one thrive and the other, despite my best efforts, just keep on in the same state? It didn't grow at all.

The church that grew and flourished had no real leadership with any notable qualifications. The unsuccessful church had talented members. There were retired pastors, an evangelist, and others. Why didn't that make the difference?

I didn't have any real church leadership experience either. What I had was a desire to have a church where people could feel safe, a church where people could go home after services with a good feeling, a church that left its attendees with a sense of spiritual refreshment, a church where visitors and members alike looked forward to returning the following week.

I had a desire for a church where people would feel at ease with their church family. I wanted a place where personal problems were a concern instead of a source of gossip. I wanted to see real interest in the church members who had a spring in their step, not members walking around like zombies.

I took the challenge and insisted that all the members adopt my rule number one. That was to make our church the safest, friendliest place to be in the area. The members all agreed, and we as a church family went to work.

The result was overwhelming. Not only did the church numbers increase, but the spirituality also grew. We all wanted that. We wanted a friendly church, not a social club. The principles that the members and I learned in that experience are priceless.

I hope some of the principles that I learned, which were such a blessing to all of us at the church, can be a blessing to you also. Does your church need a shot in the arm? I believe in a God who has the perfect solution to change a floundering church into a flourishing one. See how one simple rule can change an entire church, one person at a time.

May God bless you in your Christian walk.

—Rudy Hall

Chapter 1

What Is Going on with That Little Church?

"What is going on with that church?" Joan asked her husband Bill.

"I don't know. Why, what's wrong with it? It's still where it has always been for the last thirty years, isn't it?" Bill replied.

"Of course it is Bill, but look at it."

"Yeah. What about it? Did they paint it or something?"

"No," Joan stammered, "look at the cars in the parking lot."

"What about them, and where would you expect them to be?"

"I am talking about the amount of cars, not the fact that they are in the parking lot." Her voice showed frustration.

"Okay, I give up Joan. What is the big deal that there are a lot of cars in that parking lot?"

"Bill, how many times have we gone by this church in the last twenty years and have seen that many cars in the parking lot?"

"I don't know, do you?" said Bill rolling his eyes. "Wait, before you answer. What is the point? And why do you care how many cars are there? Seriously, what's your point Joan?"

"Bill, the point is I wonder what is going on. For the last twenty plus years you would be lucky to see five cars at the church. The last couple of months there have been at least twenty-five cars there every week. Something has changed; there are at least five times the number of people. I was just wondering what has made the difference."

"Actually you're right," Bill replied. "I guess I really didn't pay any attention, but now that I think of it, you're right. There are a lot more cars there. Maybe there is a different pastor, or some kind of recruiting push is going on. I really don't know, but something is definitely different."

"Bill, I realize that isn't our church, but our church could sure use a shot in the arm. We seem to be losing members every week. Remember when the church was growing years ago? It was inspiring to see new faces and feel their excitement."

"Yes, it was Joan, but that was a long time ago. People move for different reasons like a new job, family, and many other reasons. Also people die, or just plain give up on church, so to see a church lose members is not unusual."

"That's right," Joan replied, "But our church is not getting new members like we use to. That's the problem. Sure we are going to lose members, but when we don't replace as fast as we lose; the result will be a dead, empty church. From my view our church looks like it is on life support."

"That's right," Bill said, "but what can you do about it?"

"I don't have those answers," replied Joan, "but evidently that little church we saw awhile back figured it out. Every week the church seems full when it was close to empty for years. I just wish I knew their secret so our church could have growth like that. Success breeds success, and an illness, if not treated, usually ends in death. The point is we sure could use a little of whatever that church has in our church."

This is one sample of many similar conversations on a situation that took place in a small town in North Carolina. The participants' names are changed, but the content of the conversation is real. Many churches are in trouble. I did a search on the average American churchgoer and discovered something amazing. Most all the churches, regardless of denomination, are dwindling, and the average age of most church members has gone up to about 55 years of age.

That's a conservative figure according to the United Methodists; the average age of their members is 57 years old.[1] This is not just in the American churches. The Church of England reports "Average age of churchgoers is 61."[2]

That means there are fewer and fewer young people becoming church members. So when the older members pass away and are not replaced by younger ones, the math isn't too hard to figure out. The membership is going to get smaller and smaller.

Church after church is failing. Just down the street from my house where I have lived for twenty years is a good-looking country church. I was surprised and saddened to go home one evening after work and see a "For Sale" sign in front of the church. Even though it wasn't my church, it still hit me pretty hard. This is happening all too often.

That is why the couple was so surprised when they saw a dying church flourishing or being brought back to life. Now, we are going to go back to the church being resurrected and see how that happened. Regardless of what some might think, a church doesn't die naturally or by accident. Something causes its death. The same is true when a church flourishes; something is making it flourish.

I want to start by saying that I realize every church isn't the same. What made this church flourish is not a cure all for all floundering churches. However, there are some principles that, if ignored, will be a cancer to a church or any other organization.

---

1 Kathy L. Gilbert, "Bishops seek younger church membership by 2019," The people of The United Methodist Church, http://www.umc.org/site/apps/nlnet/content3.aspx?c=lwL4KnN1LtH&b=5259669&ct=7650221 (accessed December 10, 2012).

2 Andy Bloxham and Martin Beckford, "Average age of churchgoers now 61, Church of England report finds," *The Telegraph*, http://www.telegraph.co.uk/news/religion/7054097/Average-age-of-churchgoers-now-61-Church-of-England-report-finds.html (accessed December 10, 2012).

Chapter 2

Failure: The First Step to Success

I had just moved to North Carolina, found a church in the area, and started attending with my family. The pastor was a very nice man and had a way of making us feel welcomed. The church had about 150 members. On a good day we had about half who would show up to worship. That is fairly normal in my experience. There are always a lot more on the church books than in the church pews. We had the same schedule as most churches: teaching, singing, and preaching. Usually everything went fine, and I would go home, feeling pretty good about my day in church.

In a short time the pastor asked me to be an elder, and after prayer and soul-searching, I accepted. This pastor had two churches, the 150-member church I just mentioned, and a small church that had approximately twelve people showing up. (This is not the church mentioned in the first chapter.) This small church was around thirty minutes away from the larger church, so the pastor had his hands full dealing with two churches every week.

One day he asked me if I would speak for the main service in the small church. I said that I would and was anxious to help where I could. This wasn't my first speaking engagement, so I began to prepare as usual. I studied the passages that I wanted to present, asking the Holy Spirit to guide my thoughts, and making final notes so I was ready to go.

I arrived at the church on time and met with the church elders so that I could get acquainted with their system of doing things.

The head elder of that church gave me the usual information on how they do things, so we would both be on the same page. Then the elder said something that startled me.

"By the way young man, there is one more thing that you should know."

He went on to tell me that he was a retired pastor with more than 40 years of service. He also mentioned that even though they were a small congregation, they were all experienced.

"We have medical missionaries here and a retired evangelist. The point I'm making young man is I doubt that you will teach us anything today," he said.

"Wow! Where did that come from?" I thought.

I have been speaking all over for more than twenty years, and I have never been received like that in my life. I changed the subject for a moment and then asked him a question.

"Sir, do you have the main prayer for the congregation just before my sermon?"

"Yes," he replied.

I went on, asking, "Do you ask for the Holy Spirit to guide the thoughts of the speaker?"

Again, his answer was "yes."

Then I asked, "Do you believe your prayers are heard and answered?"

"Absolutely, I believe that," he said.

"Well sir, do you think that you and your experienced people can learn anything from the Holy Spirit?"

That ended the conversation. I spoke, and the sermon went well. Then I went home.

It was strange speaking to only ten or twelve people. The church could probably hold 120 comfortably, so it looked quite empty. I had a forty-five minute drive home, and thoughts were buzzing around in my head. My first thought was about what a strange comment concerning my not teaching them anything. I don't teach my own thoughts; I use the Bible.

My second thought was about why such a large church for such a small congregation. Then my third thought questioned why the average age of this congregation was about 75 years old? I had recently turned forty, but next to these people, I felt like a teenager. All in all, I thought the day went well, my speaking engagement was over, and I was moving on. I wanted to just enjoy the rest of the day and go home.

The week flew by, and before I knew it I was back in my home church. My pastor thanked me for filling in for him and asked how it went. I replied that it had gone well, but it was a little strange and seemed a little cold. I quickly added that I wasn't used to this church, and maybe instead of cold, it was just different, trying to hide my concerns and trying not to sound judgmental.

With a big smile the pastor said that he understood and that he was sorry. I wanted to be clear of his meaning, so I asked a question.

"What do you understand and what are you sorry for?"

The pastor shared that the church he sent me to had always been a challenge. He said that he realized I was trying to be nice, but he understood the cold feeling I experienced. He assured me it wasn't my imagination.

I thought, "Good, it isn't just me."

Then I asked, "What are you sorry for?"

He said he was sorry that he didn't warn me about what I was walking into. He knew the situation of the church members but struggled whether to say something or not. He shared with me that the church has been losing members for years. He seemed to be at a loss as to what to do about it. Then he said he had tried many things but so far it hadn't produced many results.

I told my pastor it wasn't as bad as all that and that I had a burden to see that little church grow. He agreed, we talked for a while, and that was the end of it. Or so I thought. Several days later the pastor called me and wanted to know if I would go visiting with him.

"Sure, where and who?" I said.

"Let's go visit some of the members from where you preached last week," he replied.

"Fine," I said.

We visited church members who went to church on a regular basis. We also visited just as many disgruntled members who used to go to that church, but for one reason or another, they had become dissatisfied and didn't attend anymore.

That was a real learning experience. Some were gracious and glad to see the pastor. Others were bitter and practically shut the door in his face. The pastor handled it well; with grace and patience. I was impressed and surprised at the same time. I still don't know what progress we made that day, but we made the rounds nevertheless. I shared again with him the burden to see life in that church.

Several weeks went by, and the pastor said he wanted to talk to me. I said that would be fine, and we set up a time to talk. He started out by saying the church I preached in needs a little help. That seemed like a strange statement; it seemed to me he was restating the obvious.

"I agree, it's a nice looking church in a great area but very few people attend," I said.

The pastor nodded, and then added how well I was received by the people we visited. I thanked him but began to wonder just where he was going with this. The pastor went on to say he thought that someone with my skills might just be what it takes to help that church. I explained that I really didn't know about that since they didn't seem so positive when I spoke there. He assured me that was just their way.

"Don't worry," he said, "I think it will be a great experience for you and the congregation."

I told the pastor: "I will have to pray about it."

A short time later the pastor asked me if I had been talking with my family and praying about the situation. I told him I was but that I didn't have a clear answer yet. He then shared that he had recently had a board meeting with that small church. At the meeting he presented a possible plan for me to speak a couple of times a month and work with the people to build up the church if they were interested.

I was surprised and asked, "What did they say?"

He told me that they were excited about the plan and would love to see the church grow. I was happy to hear that, so I told the pastor that was great news.

"So with that information, let's work together and build this church up," he said.

I agreed. I was pumped up and ready to start.

I knew that I didn't have formal training in this field as far as going through the seminary. I did have lots of experience in working with people. I had been giving Bible studies for several years by then. I had been preaching on a regular basis for more than ten years, so I had that experience behind me. Also, I had experience in running a successful business, which I believe is very important. In short, I believed that what I didn't have in the seminary I made up for in common sense and real-life experience. With the pastor's help, what could go wrong?

With excitement and energy, I got started. I would preach when the pastor asked and visit the people when I had time. One lady, who had been in the church for a couple of years, was excited at the prospect of seeing their little group grow. She wanted a better, more loving feeling among one another. In her opinion there was way too much bickering and too many hard feelings for a healthy church atmosphere.

As I noted earlier, there were nearly as many disgruntled members, who because of hurt feelings didn't attend church, as there were members who went to church. This lady wanted to do something to change that. She had an idea that during the few minutes between the morning program and the main service (approximately 15 minutes), it would be nice to visit just a little.

This church had a kitchen in it. So she would set out a few glasses of juice for those who wanted refreshments. She felt any newcomers could get acquainted and be welcomed by the members. If anyone wanted to go into the sanctuary and meditate or do something else in those few minutes, that would be fine too. With only ten to twelve people attending, it wasn't much of a problem as far as I could see. It wasn't my call anyway, but I thought it was a nice gesture. At least someone was doing something.

After one or two weeks of her implementing her plan, the juice stopped. She no longer attended church as regularly, and I wondered what the problem could be. I decided I would make it a point to talk to her, and try to see if there was a problem. When she did attend, she didn't seem to be as excited as before. She seemed to just be going through the motions. Finally, I had a good opportunity to talk to her.

"Hey how is everything going?" I asked her.

"Fine," she answered unemotionally.

"Well, smile a little when you say that."

She smiled, and the ice was broken.

"By the way, what happened to the juice program?"

All of a sudden the smile was gone. Her smile was replaced by hurt and maybe a little anger.

I thought to myself, "Uh oh." I was almost afraid of what she might say next. In my mind I was thinking, "Could I have done something to upset her?"

She started sharing with me and fighting off the tears at the same time.

"The reason I stopped the juice program was several of the church leaders got on my case."

"About what?" I asked.

Her voice shaking a bit she began to explain. "Some came to me and asked what I thought I was doing. I told them that I was trying to make everyone feel welcome. Then they said, 'It looks like you're trying to turn our church into a party. We don't need that here,' they exclaimed."

She continued, "All I was trying to do was make people feel comfortable and give everyone a chance to meet for a couple of minutes."

She went on to explain that she had no intention of having a party or lowering the reverence of the service. She was very hurt. There was absolutely no tact or love in the way she was dealt with.

I felt sorry for her and didn't see a problem in what she was doing anyway. That, of course, isn't the point. What I thought or didn't think isn't really the issue. The issue was the uncaring and hurtful way it was handled. She didn't have balloons and whistles, just a four-ounce cup of juice for those that wanted it.

Just to be clear, church leaders have to lead. It matters what takes place in God's house; it matters a lot. The leaders have a big responsibility to keep it a "house of prayer," not a "den of thieves" (Matthew 21:13). This, I clearly understand. Nonetheless, "how" a leader leads is many times more important than the leading itself. Is it done in love? If love is left out, then only open, cold rebuke remains. The result is usually people leaving and going somewhere else. They can get a cold shoulder and put down in the world. Why would they go to church for that? That is exactly the case with this lady; she left.

The few members, who were there, if asked, would all say they wanted the church to grow. The problem was that it seemed like they only wanted it to grow if the few who remained could be cloned. In other words if you were not just like them, you didn't feel welcome. If your thoughts were slightly different than theirs, you felt unimportant.

There was a feeling that suggesting something different or if you were a little unusual would cause the leaders to pray for fire to come down from heaven and burn you up (see Luke 9:54). Sadly, we lost yet another member who we could ill afford to lose. The challenge was discovering what could be done to change this way of thinking.

I could write this whole book on similar stories, but the point is there are reasons why some churches grow and some don't. The pastor of this church told me about a church board meeting that was opened with prayer, asking for God's love and direction from the Holy Spirit for unity, and then ended quite differently. During the meeting one board member disagreed with another one and challenged him to a fist fight in the parking lot. This is from aged, experienced leaders—not too much love and unity there.

The harder I tried the more resistance I ran into. One night at a church meeting, things were told to me that to say the least were shocking, and I don't shock easily. We were discussing a possible direction for growth. During the discussion one of the members asked me what I was trying to do here anyway.

"Help the church grow."

I went on to say, "It is my understanding that in a board meeting the pastor had already established that several months ago.

"As far as I knew, you were all on board with that. Why all the questions on what I am trying to do?"

Some at the meeting replied that in their little group they had plenty of qualified members. For example, they stated for the second time they had a retired pastor, retired evangelist, medical missionaries, and more.

They continued to show their discontent by telling me they were not happy with the pastor. I was surprised and asked, "Why is that?"

The answer was they were unhappy that I was there in the first place. According to what the pastor told me, the board was excited to have someone helping the church to grow. According to some of the board members, the pastor was pushing someone on them to help the church grow. That someone evidently was me!

What was obvious to me was we had a classic case of "failure to communicate." As if that wasn't bad enough, since they were on a roll, they had more to explain. I was told that I wasn't their Savior, and they didn't need someone to put them on the map. I didn't even reply because I was stunned. All I did was visit and talk to newcomers when they came and try to make everyone feel welcome.

Remember, only two or three did most the talking, but in a church of ten or twelve people, those few represented about twenty-five percent. My silence must have spoken volumes because soon they calmed down. With an apologetic tone they said, "It is not really you; it is the pastor. He is the one to blame. He should just let us run our own church. We are doing fine without anyone's help."

I still didn't speak but thought to myself: "Doing fine? Yeah, you're doing fine, all twelve of you. I guess if doing fine means starting out with close to thirty, and then ten years later, with all your 'fine doings' you have twelve. Then you're doing just fine."

I don't remember everything that went on after that, and it's not even the point or important. Many of the members who didn't take part in the discussion apologized for the way I was treated. Once again, it wasn't important. I could not help but think all that talent and no growth, no active Bible studies. During the time I was there, they did not do much if any evangelistic work, but they were doing fine. The question I wanted to ask but didn't was, "What is fine?"

The pastor and many of the church members encouraged me to carry on. There is a time, however, when you have to "shake off the dust from your feet" and move on (Matthew 10:14). When the church isn't behind their own success, it is a difficult thing. Change is very difficult, but when someone is satisfied with their condition, in my opinion, change is impossible.

It wasn't only difficult on me but also my family. We talked it over as a family and decided that we needed to move on. To this day I don't know what went on in the board meeting between the pastor and board members. Were they on the same page to start with or not? Did they really tell the pastor they wanted me there? Did they disagree with the pastor's wishes, but he pushed it through anyway? I will never know exactly what went on.

All I know is failure is difficult to take, especially when all you want is to see others brought to Christ. You may feel trampled on and abused. In my case I thought my job was over. I tried but couldn't pull it off. Discouragement was getting the best of me. As far as I was concerned, the whole thing was one big failure. Little did I know that God had a different plan. In His plan this failure was just the first step to success.

Chapter 3

A Visit Causes Change

I continued to stay in the larger church with the same pastor who had put me to work in his smaller church. I still had responsibilities and duties in the larger church, so I attended there full time. Although I was pretty much done licking my wounds, some of the pain from rejection and disrespect for me and my family remained. Time heals all wounds, and things eventually returned to normal.

Typically things in life change, and this was no exception. Our pastor, I enjoyed working with so much, took a call to another church and left. We have remained great friends ever since. He seemed to have a way that many people were attracted to. Some, like in most every case, were not. I guess it's true that you really can't please everybody.

The pastor who was sent to take his place was much different. Instead of making people feel that their input was important, many people felt it was his way or the highway. I was one of those people. The bottom line was around thirty people took the highway. I was not one of those people. I stayed, but I was just as unhappy as those who left.

When I first moved to North Carolina, I met a man who lived in my area and went to a different church than I did. His name was Mike; we were of the same denomination but different churches. He often asked me to transfer my membership to his church. I told him that I had many duties in my church, and the pastor used me a lot to help him. In other words I felt needed where I was at.

He would just say, "Okay, but just remember you are always welcome."

I would thank him, and we would walk and talk together. We became great friends. He had a wife and two children, who were a little younger than my children. We seemed to have a lot in common. We seemed to have similar values and enjoyed the same activities, so we kept in touch whenever we could.

One day I was at home with my family when someone drove up our drive. This was an event because I lived way out in the sticks. My driveway was a mile-long, dirt road that was uphill all the way. Not many visitors stopped by. I never even saw Jehovah's Witnesses, and I thought they went everywhere. When I went to the door to see who it was, there stood my friend Mike.

"Hey there," Mike said.

"What's up, Mike?" I asked.

He told me he just stopped by with some friends. I think the world of Mike, but no one just "stopped by" with friends at my house. To start with it is too hard to get to. Anyway, I said, "Well, come in."

He and his friends came in, and we sat down. He then introduced me to everyone he brought with him.

"Rudy," Mike said, "this is my friend and pastor. This is his wife, and these are his children."

We all said our hellos, and I was wondering why my friend was bringing a pastor to my house. Mike continued to tell me that his pastor had gone to see him and his family. Then Mike explained that he suggested to his pastor that they all go to my house to say hello.

"The pastor thought that would be great, so here we are," Mike said.

"Wonderful," I responded.

We had some small talk for a while about family and occupation, age of our children, all the normal stuff. Then Mike or his pastor said something like, "I'm sure you are busy at your church, but we would love to have you and your family at ours."

"Now I know why Mike brought the pastor over," I thought.

Mike sat there with a big grin on his face. I told them I would think about it.

I have always been pretty loyal to my church. Changing isn't easy for me or a family, so normally the answer would be "no," but a perfect storm was brewing. First, the pastor I liked so well and worked with had left for anther church. By itself that is no big deal it happens all the time. It is just harder when you just click and become not only a church worker but also a friend.

The second part of the storm was that the new pastor was hard to work with. Many of the other members who held an office felt the same way. Third, many people had left the church, most of whom I knew well; they were friends, and their leaving left a hole in the church. Fourth, I had a friend who cared enough to keep inviting me to his church. Fifth, part of this storm was my current pastor never came to visit me and my family. Yet, I was visited by a pastor who wasn't even mine.

I'll probably mention this again because it is so important, but visiting people makes a big difference. There is something about someone caring enough to take the time to visit. As a pastor or elder you have many responsibilities. For example there is preaching, you may be good at it, you may not. Counseling same thing, some are better than others. The list could go on. Of all the things that a pastor or elder has to do, the key is visiting. Just think about it. Visiting is a way to form friendships. I am much more likely to listen to a speaker if he is a friend of mine. It is the same with counseling if you trust him as you do a friend; you may listen a little more. Being a friend does something else; it can cover a multitude of mistakes.

For example, I have given many Bible studies. I do not have golden oratory, so I will probably say something sometime that comes out wrong. If you make a mistake with a friend, he or she is less likely to take it in a wrong way. He or she will probably just laugh at you and give you a hard time because of your friendship. That doesn't come by accident, it comes by visiting.

The perfect storm or conditions were set; I accepted their invitation and joined my friend's church. It was a new beginning. I knew some people there, but for the most part they were all new to me. It was nice to go to a church and have no responsibilities except to sit there and listen to the pastor.

The pastor who came to visit me left for another church about the time I changed churches. The next pastor was great. He was personable, organized, and seemed to know what he was doing. I said it was nice to have no responsibilities for a change, but that didn't last too long. When an organized person that knows what he is doing, like this new pastor did, he not only gets to work, but he also puts anyone to work who is willing.

In a very short time after joining the church, I was once again an elder with responsibilities. I felt the elders and pastor made a good team along with the rest of the church officers. Once again, it was enjoyable to go to church. There seemed to be a spirit of teamwork.

Pastors have tried all kinds of ways to draw people to their church. Elders, deacons, and members in general have gone to great lengths to fill the pews. Many churches have a bingo night, thinking that since casinos are busy all the time, they ought to try that. Many bring in a powerful speaker from out of town, thinking that'll do it. Many have had a scare tactic, for example, they preach fire and brimstone or the old "turn or burn" sermons. Some try guilt: "Jesus died for you man! What are you doing for Him?"

Bingo night works on bingo night. By the way I read an article where the church raffled off a case of fine wine. The raffle was a success, but the people left when the wine did. Powerful speakers get people in the front door but they leave through the back door. They stir up a storm with their motivating preaching, but when they leave and the dust settles, the high emotion is gone and soon so are the people.

Preachers know what I am talking about. My brother went to an evangelistic crusade by a fantastic speaker. Many gave their hearts to the Lord, including him. In fact, 140 people made a decision for Christ and joined him in baptism. One year later, four remained in the church. Most of the people left within a few weeks. By God's grace my brother stayed firm and is furthering God's work today.

There is no end to the schemes to draw people into the church. Millions of dollars are spent each year in evangelism, and that's fine as it has its place. Scare tactics work at best for a short time. Guilt doesn't form a relationship with Christ, and without that, what's the point anyway?

Christ was the best evangelist ever; let's look at a tactic of His. "The Lord has appeared of old to me, saying: 'Yes, I have loved you with an everlasting love; therefore with *lovingkindness* I have drawn you'" (Jeremiah 31:3, emphasis added).

Just in case you missed this passage, God's Word uses the term "lovingkindness" another thirty-one times just to get the point across. That's how the Lord draws people.

Pure kindness that doesn't expect to be paid back is priceless. Sometimes that can be quite involved, sometimes just a kind word or a smile. It might be an encouraging phone call in the middle of the week. It could be a simple card that in one way or another says, "I appreciate you." It could be many things to many people. To me it was simply a visit with a message that said, "You are valuable, and we would love to have you be part of this group."

Chapter 4

Been There, Done That

As I mentioned earlier, the new pastor put his members to work. I, along with a few of the other elders, would speak in the pastor's absence. This pastor also had two churches. One church had 120 members, with about sixty showing up on a regular basis. The second church had about thirty people on the books, with about eight showing up on a regular basis.

One day the pastor said he wanted to talk to me. As it turned out, he was going to be out of town and needed a speaker for the small church. I said I would and went through the normal preparations, and by the end of the week, I was ready to speak.

The church was small and oddly shaped, not your typical-looking church. The sanctuary could hold maybe sixty people at the most. When I arrived, there were only a couple cars in the parking lot. I was hoping that I had the correct address. If I did, I couldn't help but think, "Where is everybody?"

I went inside the church and recognized one couple from a church I had attended several years before. Counting the two of them, there were maybe eight people in all. I asked the couple, "Is this it?"

"Probably," they replied.

I thought, "Wow! This is even smaller than the other small church I spoke at."

I have spoken in churches with memberships of 500, maybe more. In a large church with 500–1,000 people, it can be difficult at times. When you look out, if you're not used to it, you feel small. The church feels big, and it takes a little getting used to.

On the other hand if the church is really small especially twelve or fewer, that can be even harder. You may not think so, but it is. It is almost like preaching to your family at the dinner table. Talking to them would be easy, but preaching a sermon to a group of that size can be difficult.

That day at church went fine. I spoke, and the few who were there seemed to really enjoy it. I had an invitation for lunch from the couple I knew and had an enjoyable afternoon. The dinner was great, and we caught up on some old times, and the whole day seemed to be great.

After dinner and the normal conversation, the couple asked me what I thought of their church. I thought to myself, "Regarding what? The outside and inside of the church could use some paint and repairs. Only eight to ten people show up on a regular basis. What am I suppose to think?"

I really didn't want to give this nice couple that type of answer. I replied, "It seems to be a nice little church."

They then continued and asked, "What do you think of the people?"

I said, "Well, I guess they were fine."

That answer wasn't really true. I mean it was partly true. The two who were asking the question were great. I didn't know the others, but most of the others appeared a little strange. All in all, the answer, "Well, I guess they were fine," was probably the best answer.

The next question they asked was an easier question: "What do you think of little churches in general?"

I instantly replied that typically I like them. There is more involvement with the members in a small church. In a small church everybody has to help simply because there are fewer people. I went on to say that it was exciting to see growth in a small church.

Growth is more noticeable. For example, in a large church of say 600 members, if you get ten more members, you would barely notice it. In this small church of eight to ten members, ten new members would double the active membership. That would be exciting to see twice as many people as were there the previous week.

Then this couple asked me if I would be willing to help them build up this church. I immediately thought to myself: "No way!" I didn't say it, but I sure thought it. I did say, "Listen, I really would like to see this church grow, but I don't think I'm your man."

They explained that they disagreed, saying, "I think you would be just what this church needs. You have energy, business experience, and in general good, common sense."

My mind was not in tune with what they were saying. Sure they were being nice and complimentary, but to myself I was saying, "No way, I am just not interested."

I started sharing with them without going into a lot of detail. "You guys are great, and you have a great mission. I realize you have a burden to see the church grow, and that's great. I have already tried to build up a small church, and it ended in a train wreck. It was a bad experience for me and my family, and it is a lot harder than you think. I just don't think it's a good idea for me to tackle something like that. In layman's terms I've been there and done that."

This couple was really determined. "The fact that you have tried just means that you have experience. Besides that, if not you, who would you suggest for the job? Over the past twenty years we have had several pastors, and they have all tried. They were all pretty good pastors, but they just didn't have the time or skill or something to make it happen."

With that being said, they added, "We don't want to make a hardship on you or your family. If you're not interested, we understand. We just believe that you might just have what it takes to make this happen. Would you at least think about it, pray about it, talk with your family, and let us know what you decide?"

I had to say, "Yes, I will pray about it."

As a Christian, there is really no other answer but "yes" when it comes praying about something. Any major decision should start with prayer. Of course, if we do that, we need to be honest and listen to that still, small voice mentioned in 1 Kings 19:12. If we ask God, He will answer. When He answers, we need to listen.

Most of us know the story of Jonah. God told Him to go to Nineveh, but Jonah wasn't comfortable with that. To him it made a lot more sense to go to Tarshish. Jonah tried as hard as he could to have his own way, but he ended up in the belly of a great fish for three days. Finally, he went to Nineveh where he was told to go, but it sure would have been better just to have listened in the first place.

I did go home to talk with my family and pray about it. Not all that earnestly, or at least as earnestly as I should have. The problem was I just didn't want to go through another bad experience. Then I remembered stories of the disciples and others who followed the Lord's leading no matter what.

The persecution they went through was amazing. Some were thrown into prison, and when they got out, they went back to preaching and doing the same things that put them in prison in the first place. Those stories and many more made my ordeal seem pretty small.

Even people who weren't in the Bible, like Abraham Lincoln, went through many setbacks. If you google "failures of Abraham Lincoln," you will see the many setbacks he had on the way to the presidency. Almost every successful person has had setbacks. Christians should expect setbacks and problems and not run from them. Much of Matthew 10 is dedicated to the cost of discipleship. Jesus never promised an easy life to those who serve Him.

With all that and much more, I spent time thinking about what I should do. I did pray about it, but didn't hear any booming voice. My family was surprisingly positive. I'm not saying they were excited, but at least they were open and not negative about it.

The decision to help this church would be much bigger than before because it didn't work last time. That may not bother some people, but it did me. I have been successful in most everything

I set out to do. Whether it is business, Bible studies, or anything else, I am usually successful. Failure stings a little bit, but when it affects my family, it is much worse.

The Bible says that making your own decision can be dangerous or unsafe. "In the multitude of counselors there is safety" (Proverbs 11:14). I have found that to be true. The key is asking the right people for counsel. Many times we ask our friends who may not be qualified in helping, but they tell us what we want to hear. That may be nice, but it is not sound counsel.

I decided to run this idea past a co-elder and my friend Mike. Mike seemed to be focused on what was right or wrong, not feelings. I believed that he would give me good counsel based on God's principles. I met with him and to make a long story short, he said, "What an undertaking."

He was aware of the little church also and knew it would be a challenge. Nevertheless, in conclusion he said he believed that I should give it a try.

The more I thought and prayed about it, my mood was changing. I was going from "no way" to "what if." I was thinking about what if I was to do this. The last time I prayed and put my heart and soul into it, it failed. If I were to do it again, what would make this time different? Praying and putting my heart and soul into it wasn't enough. There had to be more to it than that. My focus became if I did this, what would I do to make the result different?

After much prayer and thought I decided that I would honor my friends' request from the small church. However, I would only tackle this job under certain conditions. If those conditions were met, then I would take that as a sign to move forward. If those conditions were not met, all bets were off. I went to my friends and told them I would try to work with their church under certain conditions. I explained what those were, and they felt there would be no problems.

No problems? What planet were they living on? Almost everybody, including pastors, I talked to thought this was a worthy cause. At the same time they thought I was crazy because in their eyes it was almost impossible. After all, several qualified pastors and twenty years of good intentions that failed didn't make a recipe for positive thinking. I had to get the "been there and done that" thought out of my mind. The new thinking had to be "go there and do that, but do it differently, and this time be successful."

Chapter 5

A Time for Decision and Direction

Running a successful business for years teaches a person a thing or two. I have known a few pastors who have come from a business background, and in almost every case they make a better pastor. For one thing in business, at the end of the year you look at what you did well and keep doing it. You also look at what didn't work, assess why it didn't do well, and make the necessary changes. If you don't do that, then you will not have a business very long.

Those pastors with a business background find the same principle holds true with the job of running a church. When you are successful at something, keep doing it. If you have a situation that went badly, find out why, and make adjustments. Sometimes pastors and leaders without business backgrounds don't do that; here is one reason why. In business if you don't do that, you will go broke. Unsuccessful pastors, on the other hand, may just get placed in another church. Most times the bigger the downside or loss, the faster we learn.

It was natural for me to take a hard look at what went wrong, and right off the bat, I noticed something. In the first attempt to help the church grow, I was asked by the pastor, not the people. That may sound small, but I don't think it is. If I took this challenge, that would be the first change I would make. I would call a meeting and invite all the church members and the pastor.

At that meeting I would agree to work with them to help them build their church only if they all agreed. That way there would be no more: "the pastor told us one thing, and he told you something else." There would be no more: "what are you doing here anyway." There would be no more: "Why are you trying to put us on the map? What's in it for you?" In short, the church members would have to be completely on board with everything.

Before the meeting with the church, I would have a private meeting with the pastor. The pastor would be a big key to the success or failure of this program. I have seen church members moving one way, and the pastor trying to pull them in a different direction. That never works very well. People all have one thing in common—they all have their strengths and weaknesses. Pastors are people to; they also have their strengths and weaknesses.

Pastors at times are afraid to let someone lead out in a project like this. The pastors are afraid that it could blow up in the lay person's face, and it could make things worse instead of better. Pastors may feel that if the project worked very well, they may lose influence with the people. There are all sorts of reasons why a pastor would be hesitant to let a person go with a project like this.

As you can imagine, I was a bit nervous talking to the pastor about this project. To my surprise there was no opposition at all; he was fine with it. His attitude was to "go for it". In fact, he was so positive that he made me nervous. I thought to myself, "Why is he so positive? What does he know that I don't?"

We had a great meeting. He warned me that it was a great undertaking, and it would be a hard thing to accomplish. I told him that I understood, and I didn't expect it to be easy.

When I was asked to work with this church, I truly believed that I would get out of it. First, as I have mentioned, I didn't want to do it. I tried before, had a bad experience, and had moved on. The problem with these thoughts was if this was God's will, I didn't want to work against God. I thought that when I took my plan to the pastor, he would be a roadblock to the plan. I figured he would say, "It's a good idea, but let's do it this way."

I would then be off the hook because I felt there needed to be a different plan. The plan we had was the plan that had been tried for the last twenty years and had produced little to no results. Still, in many cases the pastor is hesitant to let go of the reins.

When the pastor said to "go for it," not only was it a surprise, but it also eliminated the first excuse that was in my head. I could no longer say that we as the members could decide on a plan that could be successful, but the pastor will probably not allow it. This pastor had an unexpected attitude: if you have a plan, and the church is behind it and will work together to build up the church, you have my blessing.

Only one hurdle was left: the church members. I decided in my mind that if I had a meeting with the church members, they would all have to agree. If even one person voted not to do this, I would scrap the plan and be off the hook. Even though there were only a few members, getting everybody to agree on anything isn't easy.

The pastor set a date for a constituency meeting, which included all members. They all had plenty of time to make arrangements to be there. They were all notified of the meeting. No one could say he or she didn't know or didn't have time to be there. I also asked the pastor for a favor. I asked him not to be the pastor at this meeting.

He asked what I meant. I said that I wanted him to call the meeting but not promote the program. Instead, I wanted him to sit with the members and be one of them during my presentation. I added that after the meeting I would like him to give comments or ask questions just like any other member. That was fine with him. I think he actually enjoyed it, maybe even a little too much.

The night of the meeting arrived; the pastor introduced me, although most everyone knew me anyway. I was the guy from the other church who preached once in a while. I began by telling them that I would keep the meeting short. I continued to tell them: "As you know, there have been many empty pews for a very long time. All of us could almost fit into one or two pews during any given service. I would like to see us, as the members, change that.

I told them that I believed that we could if we all had the same goal. It's usually easy to have the same goal. On a sports team, let's say football, all the players generally have the same goal. They all want to win as winning is normally their goal. However, wanting to win is just part of it. Without a plan, winning is usually just a wish. We needed to want to win and to follow a winning plan to make it happen. If we did that, we could fill the pews.

I had a really simple plan that had only two rules. Rule number one: make this church a safe place to come to, make it an enjoyable place to be. Members and visitors needed to want to come back next week. This church must be a place where they can forget their problems and maybe even solve a few. This should not be a place where they get more problems. Whatever their religious beliefs, color, creed, status, background, etc., they were to feel welcomed.

If you have a problem with someone, try as hard as you can to leave it in your car before you enter the church. I am not changing Matthew 18, which explains if you have a problem go to that person and work it out if you can. It doesn't say go to them and work it out when you get in church. Rule number one sounds easy, but evidently it isn't. I say that because if it was followed, I believe all our churches would be filled. In short, rule number one is to make this church the safest, most enjoyable church in the area, not only for worship but also to enjoy Christian fellowship with one another.

I went on for a short time, explaining this very simple principle, and then I opened it up for questions. The pastor was great; he was supportive without being arm-bending. He understood this needed to be the people's decision based on what they wanted to do, not their decision based on what the pastor wanted them to do.

The questions came in and some were quite interesting. Remember, other than the one "train wreck," I didn't have any experience in building up a church membership. Here are a few examples of the questions.

>Question: Have you ever been trained to do this so-called church building?

Answer: No, not really, I have seen these principles work, and the lack of them causes problems, decreases membership, and promotes discouragement.

Question: Do you have any credentials of any kind, like pastor or something?

Answer: Again, no.

Question: Have you been through the seminary or taken any college courses?

Answer: Once again, no. Listen, I really have had no formal training of any kind. However, I believe that growing a church is more about being kind and compassionate toward one another and using other simple, Bible-based principles that are tried and proven.

Question: As you know, we are a small church and have been that way for some time. We used to have a lot more members, but years ago there was a split, and this is what we are down to. We have had several pastors, probably four, five, or more in the past twenty years or so. We have had some good pastors, and we have a good one now. They all have said that they had hopes for this church to grow and the pews to be filled. That hasn't happened so far. The question is what makes you able to do this with no real qualifications when it hasn't happened so far?

Answer: Once again, it's going to take more than a person's qualifications or college degree in my opinion to fill this church. Not one of the pastors this church has had has lacked in education. All of them have been through the seminary. Where has that gotten this church? It will be the love of Christ in us revealed to others that will make the difference.

	Our current pastor has two churches, and this is the smallest one. He has many responsibilities, board meetings, finance meetings, reports to the conference, evangelistic meetings, and much more. All we have to do is be kind and loving and show the spirit of Christ in all we do, and I believe the pews will be filled. I know this sounds too simple, but I know it will work.
Question:	You have spent a lot of time on "rule number one." You said there were two rules. What is rule number two?
Answer:	Rule number two is never forget rule number one.
	I might ask, "What is the downside?" We only have eight or ten coming anyway. Most of us know that our conference has been thinking of closing this little church. The question to me is not what are our chances of winning with this program? The better question is what do we have to lose? Don't ask me if I feel I'm better than all the pastors who have tried this. My answer is that I'm not. But you might ask yourself by looking around at the size of this group: "How much worse can he be?"
Question:	Will you move your membership to this church or leave it where it is until you see what happens here?
Answer:	If I didn't believe in this, I wouldn't be here. My membership, my family, and my focus will be here.

There were other questions, but I don't really remember all of them. These were the ones that stuck out to me. When we were all done discussing the issues, I told the group to talk it over with the pastor, let him know the decision, and then he would let me know. I wanted to give them time to discuss it for themselves.

Chapter 6

First Order of Business

The next day the pastor informed me that they had made a unanimous decision, and it was "yes." The pastor's duties didn't change much. Prior to the meeting the pastor would be at the church to speak every other week because he had two churches. When he wasn't there, he would find someone to preach. The only change in this respect was he didn't have to get anyone because I did it. He was still there every other week. My life, on the other hand, changed quite a bit.

For me this was where the rubber met the road. I had rallied the members to think we could actually do something with this church. This was the time to prove it. I had been taught from childhood that if you're going to say something, back it up. I believed in this, prayed about it, and then it was time to get to work.

I had said earlier that one difference between the two churches—the one that failed in the beginning and this one—was the support. The first time I had the support of the pastor, not so much from the members. This time it was unanimous between both the members and pastor.

Another difference was the people. The background of several of the members in the first church was one of experience. For example, I mentioned a retired pastor, a retired evangelist, a medical missionary, and a church school teacher. This was not the case in the second church. With this church it was a different crowd—if eight can be called a crowd. There were no real church leaders with professional experience or professional education.

That included me. I had a small town, public high school education. As far as church or religious education, I am a G.E.D. (God Educated Disciple). On paper if the last church failed, this one didn't stand a chance. I felt differently; this wasn't on paper. I felt that by ourselves we would fail for sure, but "with men this is *impossible*, but with *God all* things are *possible*" (Matthew 19:26, emphasis added).

Just like a business, when you have a job to do, you look at the job and look at the people you have to work with and get busy. First of all, there were my two friends and their daughter who got me into this in the first place. They ran a little rustic furniture business. They would make the rustic, natural furniture and sell it where they could and did well at it. My friends came to church with her brother and sister-in-law. He was a painter, and she worked in real estate.

Then there was this couple who always sat in the same place. If they had an opinion on something, they would let you know. Good or bad you knew just where they stood. As far as that goes, everyone knew exactly where they stood with them. There are people like them in almost every church who think they are appointed the "spiritual sheriffs." If they think that someone is not as spiritual as they should be, it is their duty as sheriff to inform those at fault.

Then there was this very sweet elderly woman. I think she had spent her life in the church. She loved music and could play the piano well. She also could and did play by ear although I think she may have been suffering from dementia. She would get up to play when the church sang. The song may be "What a Friend We Have in Jesus," but half way through she would change it to "Bringing in the Sheaves" or something else. The members would obviously be confused, so they would mumble whatever words seemed appropriate to them at the time. Needless to say song service was painful at times.

One man was maybe thirty-five or more; I never knew. He was mentally challenged but a nice person. He walked to church, sometimes our church or sometimes another church. Whenever a member saw him walking, he or she would give him a ride to church, and someone would always take him home. He became an every weak attendee.

During the church service if he felt like praying or saying something about what was playing on CBS, NBC, or other channels, he would. It didn't matter what part of the service we were in. He would just stand up and let his thoughts go. He was harmless but a little distracting, especially if I was preaching at the time. We all understood, so I would pause my sermon for a moment until he finished and then proceed. I believe he always felt welcome in our little church. He was a product of rule number one.

Another attendee was this lady who lived by herself. One of the members always picked her up and took her home after the service. She was at the point in her life when that was almost impossible; she needed some supervision. She would leave the stove burners on as well as other dangerous things in her apartment.

In church she would sit there for a little while, and on occasion she would go to the church kitchen. She would then come back to the sanctuary with something to eat. It might be a little ice cream or a tub of butter. Someone would do what they could to assist her. Again, she was relatively harmless but definitely distracting.

There were a couple more elderly people, mostly all nice people. With all our problems, and we all had them, we also had one goal. We all wanted the church to grow. Unlike the first church that wanted their church to grow only if the newcomers fit a particular pattern. This church wanted their church to grow, period. "If this rule number one could work here, it could work anywhere," I thought to myself.

In my construction business I had big jobs building eight to ten-thousand-square-foot homes, for example, and I had a small crew. Filling this church was a big job, and again, there was a small crew to accomplish it. Any who could and would work had to work together if this was going to be successful. My focus and goal was growing this church, but there was a secondary goal: this church could be an example and encouragement to other dwindling churches. If this church could do it, any church could.

The question was where to start? How do we get more people into this church? From where do we get them? The one thought I came up with was that maybe it would be a good idea to start with former members. That is, members who used to come and were still in the area but no longer attended.

This is a delicate process and should be handled accordingly. If you are going to visit the "I'm not coming back" people, the biggest consideration is not them. The biggest consideration is you. You probably will hear things you disagree with, like "The pastor is stupid. He doesn't care about me; he only cares about the important members, and people like me don't count."

You may hear something about a good friend of yours, like "Joe (maybe your friend) said this to me or did that, and if that's what church is all about, you can have it." You might even hear something about yourself. Something you supposedly said or did that upset them. It may be true or not. The point is to prepare yourself for some form of attack, either on you, the church you love, or someone you care about.

Normally, preparing means, if you're going to meet an attacker, take weapons. Not in this case. Prepare yourself to be quiet. Prepare yourself to listen. You have two ears and one mouth, so listen at least twice as much as you talk. Who knows, you might just learn something. Be prepared to weather the storm, not fix the storm. Remember there is a reason why they are not attending, and it usually isn't because they were so happy they just couldn't stand it anymore.

Sometimes you will see immediately that the reason that you think they're upset isn't even true. It isn't even real. Remember, perception is reality. To them it is true. To them it is real. Telling a person that their problem is not really a problem almost never works. Telling them that "so and so" didn't mean to hurt you usually never works either. If they believed that, they wouldn't have left in the first place.

The point is listen, be supportive, non-combative, and don't make excuses for everyone. Sometimes people do and say really dumb things. These things cause others to be unhappy and leave the church. Telling them those people aren't dumb isn't true and doesn't help. Remember, there are no miracle cures. Every situation is different. What works for one might be disastrous for another. "Be wise as serpents and harmless as doves" (Matthew 10:16).

With the thought of seeing the "not coming backers," one situation came up immediately. There was a man and his wife who were active in the church for years, but they had not attended for some time. I knew of them but didn't really know them very well. I had no idea why they chose to leave, but I was about to find out.

I went to their house, they invited me in, and we just had a friendly conversation for a while. Then I told them I had been attending the little church that they used to attend. I told them I missed seeing them there. They asked how everyone was doing, I said that everyone was doing fine; then they started sharing.

It seemed that someone in the church (I think it was a self appointed "sheriff") saw something that he thought was "out of order" with the self-appointed power that was given to him by himself, he made an arrest. In other words he told them that the church didn't approve of what they did and told them to "cease and desist" or in no uncertain terms to cut it out.

Others in the church didn't appreciate this couple either. They said that they were very upset at the lack of respect given them. In their minds all they did was try to help. It seemed to them the more they tried to help, the worse they were treated. They concluded that if their help wasn't appreciated, then they just wouldn't go to church anymore. Besides that, in their view the pastor hadn't even noticed that they quit going to church or didn't care because he hadn't even visited them.

"If no one wants us, we will go somewhere else."

"Wow," I thought, then I told them, "I know I'm new and don't know everyone like you do. However, I know someone who does appreciate you and would like to see you come back."

They thought a minute and asked, "Who?"

"Me," I said, "I would like you to come back. Besides I know the devil is happy when you stay home, and Christ is sad. Let's change that, please consider coming back. I believe that there is a better spirit, so please give it another try."

They sternly said, "No promises, but we'll think about it."

The short version is they did come back, felt better, were treated better, and became workers in the church. I didn't always have that same result, but there are important principles that I always used. First, I didn't tell them everybody wanted them back. They wouldn't have believed it, and neither did I. Some people were glad they were gone and hoped they would never be back. Sheriffs don't run someone out of town and then cry about it. They are actually proud of their deeds in most cases.

Second, I gave them a reason: I want you back, and I believe things will be different. Third, give them a chance to be bigger than their problems. In other words ask them to overlook the problem people, rise above it, and give it another try. These are sound principles that should always be used in one form or another. I didn't give them a quick fix or an empty promise. "Come back, and let's try together" was a better answer in this case, but all situations are different.

Just think if eight people were attending church and two more came back, we just improved the membership by twenty-five percent. I call that off to a great start. The first order of business was complete. Assemble your team members, evaluate their strengths and weaknesses, and form a plan of action.

Chapter 7

The Pastor Leaves, So What?

We had just nicely started when I received some bad news. The pastor informed the church that he had taken a call to another church. He said that it was really a family issue, and he could be closer to his family. That was really important to him. He told his larger church the same thing that he told us at the small church. He said something like, "I hope you all understand and God bless."

Some of the members in our small church were a little upset and didn't hide their feelings. They were just getting used to this pastor, and then he was leaving. They had formed a friendship with him, and they felt they were losing a friend. Disappointment was evident and morale was going downhill fast.

I didn't have the friendship tie that some of the members had. I hadn't been there that long and was busy with my construction business. When I did have some time, I was occupied with the church. This kept me so busy that I didn't really have time to build a relationship with the pastor. My disappointment was of a different sort.

My problem was the fact we had just started, and the main player was gone. He wasn't the main player as far as work goes. He was important because he was different. As I said earlier, many pastors feel they need to be in control. They feel that they have to be the coach and quarterback of the team. This guy was different. He allowed the church members to run the church, and he would serve where he would be most needed. His attitude was "How can I be of service to you guys?"

The pastor's leaving was a problem for me. Who would replace him? Would the new one be as helpful and understanding as this pastor? My opinion was based on thirty-five years of experience sitting on church boards and working with many pastors. This pastor would be hard, if not impossible, to replace. Furthermore, we at the church had little to nothing to say about it. Our church conference or headquarters sent us the new pastor; it was not up to us.

The situation was simple to evaluate. We had just started to rebuild, and the pastor was leaving. The people liked the pastor and were discouraged because he was leaving. I was discouraged because the chance of getting a similar replacement was slim. The active members came to me and asked, "What are we going to do?"

I thought for a moment because I knew I had to do something to motivate the members and take their minds off the pastor leaving, so I answered, "About what?"

"About the pastor leaving," they replied.

Shock and disgust was in their voices. To them we had just built up a little momentum, only to have this happen. The little band of concerned members continued.

"We have barely started, and now the pastor is leaving us."

"So what?" I said.

"So what!" they exclaimed, "What do you mean 'so what'?

"Listen up," I said. "I was thinking about what was going to happen to this church myself. I have listened to you saying, the church this, and the church that. I finally asked myself, 'What is the church?' The answer is that the church is us. We are the church. This building we worship in is just a building we worship in. The pastor is just one man with a job to further the gospel of Jesus Christ.

"For the last twenty years this church has dwindled because we, the church, let it dwindle. The pastors here have two churches and have tried to split their time and do their job. For years we, the church, thought our job was to watch the pastor do his job. Now we realize that we have the same job of furthering the gospel and saving souls. Instead of one person and two churches, we have several people and only one church to focus on.

"Once again, my point is 'so what.' Let's worry about our church and our jobs. Let's not worry about the pastor, and where or why he is going. He said he is doing what the Lord has led him to do. Good for him. We need to focus on what the Lord wants us to do. I believe it is building this church."

The next question was "Who will we get to replace him?"

"I really don't know, and I really don't care," I replied. I quickly added, "Before any of you have a heart attack, or think I'm crazy, let's just do our job and let the Lord do His. He will get the right person here. God knows our needs; let's leave that up to Him.

The pastor did leave a few weeks later and was missed. He was in many hearts and prayers but the work of the little church was not affected. The whole church was about twelve or more strong when he left; however, the church had a healthy attitude. In fact, looking back it was probably a good thing for us. We had already decided we could take care of our church. This was the time and the opportunity to prove it.

I want to take a moment to explain something. We did not have an arrogant or cocky attitude in our "so what" opinion. We had just decided to take ownership of who we were. We were Christians. That was to be like Christ as much as possible. He was our example; He would be our new pastor and leader.

We were without a pastor for some time. Eventually, the conference sent an interim pastor, but he was more of an interruption than a blessing. He was more focused on the larger church; I guess they needed him more. He had a long commute; so much of his time was spent driving.

The little church just kept on keeping on. Little by little we would pick up a visitor who decided to stay. Friends or relatives of members would come just to see if we were still there and what we were doing. Now and then they would be so impressed, they would stay.

After several months we got word that a new pastor was going to arrive. We would be able to meet him, but in reality whether we wanted him or not, the conference hired the pastors, not us. By this time we had grown to about twenty members. That was two-and-a-half times more than we started with, not bad for a group of misfits.

I gave everybody in the church a mission. The mission was to come to church with a search-and-shake attitude. If you came to church and didn't shake at least ten hands, you failed your mission. The leadership tried hard to have a spiritual, well-organized program. We did fine as far as that was concerned. The messages were spiritual, and we all got a blessing. That was not the only reason we came. We understood as members that we came to be a witness to others and to get spiritually fed.

We did not come to sit in the pews and be entertained. In many churches you find people saying, "That sure is a cold church." I was going to do what I could not to hear that. I would encourage all members to do the same. Shake a hand and ask each visitor where they came from. Besides, if you are shaking hands and being friendly, then it is hard to say it's a cold church. Many times it is cold people who say that it is a cold church. They may complain or say, "No one talked to me," but did they talk to anyone themselves? In most cases they did not.

We were looking forward to seeing our new pastor when he arrived, but we were getting along just fine. The little church was well on its way. It wasn't just the fact that the church was growing although that was our goal. The unexpected blessing was that we as individuals were growing. We were looking forward to meeting each other at church. If someone was gone, he or she was actually missed. If someone was sick, we actually cared. We were much more than a growing church, we were becoming a family.

CHAPTER 8

The Missing Piece

I had several plans for the success of the church. As was stated earlier, I did not go to the seminary. I had no formal training. I didn't, and still don't, know Greek or Hebrew. I haven't worked as a pastor or trained as one. None of that matters to me. In my construction business to be successful I always concentrated on what I had, not on what I didn't have.

The question was what did I have and how would that help the church. I had a love and desire for the church. The church, as stated before, is the people. To me the answer was simple: show the people that you truly do care for them. I had already talked to the "ex-members," but what about the current ones?

You don't need a degree to visit. It is pretty simple; here's how it works. Find out where someone lives, go there, and talk to them. That is all there is to it. It is amazing to me how simple it is and yet how little importance is put on it. If something is simple, costs very little, and is extremely effective, I'm all for it.

One of the first things I did when I started working to build up the church was to visit. When you visit, you see people in a different way. You see them in their regular clothes. You see their passions. For example, I went to one home and saw all kinds of canned goods.

As it turned out, this person took care of a large garden and canned much of the food the family ate. She told me all about it, and I even learned a gardening trick or two. I didn't learn too much about canning but I did go home with a jar of blackberry jam that melted in my mouth. In fact, I happened to visit that house about the time my jam ran out. It is funny how things work out that way.

On tables and shelves in their homes and on the walls were pictures of the church members' families. They loved to talk about their families. As they talked, something started to happen. A picture started to form in my mind. I started to see how they were raised, what kind of parents they had, and what struggles they went through. I saw where they started and understood where they wanted to go.

While visiting people in their homes, I had a thousand opportunities to know them in ways that would have been impossible at church. In church I saw the smiles, but when I visited, I saw what was behind that smile. Was it a true smile, or was it a cover for a hurting soul? Just spending a little time with them, and they would reach out for understanding. That's what visiting is.

Probably the biggest complaint that I have heard over the years about pastors is their lack of visiting. Even in a small church, many people hardly ever get a visit. When they do, many times it is only because there is a problem. Sometimes when an elder or pastor goes up the walk, the homeowner will wonder, "What did I do?"

The biggest key to the growth of the church I worked with was visiting. It needs to be the first priority. If you want the people to listen to your sermons a little better, visit. If you want to be taken a little more seriously as a pastor, visit. If you want to be respected, visit. You will get this and a lot more by visiting. You will not get it by your eloquent speaking nearly as easily as visiting.

I believe pastors have neglected this as a general rule. Some still visit, but most only visit if there is a problem or an emergency, like a death, divorce, etc. Those are necessary visits, but even those are much more effective if you have been visiting on a regular basis. I have had pastors tell me that they have reports to fill out each week. They have sermons to prepare, evangelistic meetings to organize, church board, school board, finance committees, and the list goes on. In short there is no time left, or so they say, to visit.

"That is too bad," I tell them, "because almost everything you mentioned would be better if you visited a little more."

I said earlier that I believe visiting should be on the top of the list, but for too many it is on the bottom. People tend to stay where they feel loved. It is hard to make them feel that way at a finance meeting. People tend to stay where they feel important and respected. That is hard to do in a board meeting. I understand it all has to get done, but if there is little importance placed on visiting, growing a church will be a difficult task.

When there is a problem with a non-growing or dwindling church, people tend to see the problem, or at least they think they do. For example, if the pastor had better sermons, it would help. If the pastor spent more time visiting, it would be a good start. Maybe if we had a better greeter, if the church was painted, if we had new carpet, and the list goes on. We all see the problems that need fixing.

We would do so much better to say, "What can I do?"

Most all of us can visit. Reach out to someone by simply going over to his or her house. A simple lunch somewhere can make a huge difference. Don't worry about the greeter, be the greeter. Don't worry about the pastor seeing people. It is your church, you see people. Always remember, it is your church, do what you can. If someone was hired to be your housekeeper, you wouldn't consider the house to be theirs. The person most concerned with your house typically is you. Try to feel the same way about your church.

Several years ago our small church had some evangelistic meetings. Flyers were sent out to every house in the county. The fundraising and the organization of the mailings was done perfectly. The pastor prepared well for the series. He was a good speaker and knew his material; his presentation was excellent and created a lot of interest. The meetings were a success as far as I'm concerned. There was some new interest in the community, so all went well.

One lady who went to these meetings lived alone in town and had a few health problems. She was interested in the materials and shared some with her church family. They warned her not to listen to the new little church she was visiting.

"They are all confused and don't care about you," said her church friends.

Her interest was aroused, so she kept coming. She wanted to do the right thing, so she asked her church family and friends about the new light she had received. Her friends and pastor would not discuss the Bible truths or doctrines with her. They only said, "Trust us; we are your friends. If you continue to listen to that or any other church, you are making a big mistake."

She really didn't know what to do. Should she go with what she learned in the Bible or go with her long-time, good friends. She started listening to their reasoning, which started to make a little sense to her. They would say, "Don't get caught up in different beliefs. God loves you, and you love Him. That's all that matters. We are the ones who care about you, not them."

Then she started feeling bad, had a checkup, and found out she needed an operation. It wasn't life-threatening but she would be in the hospital for a week or so. While she was in the hospital, one of the elders from our small church visited her. A few others did as well. This elder didn't really share anything spiritual other than having prayer before he left. She came through the surgery fine, went home, and had a full recovery.

She kept coming to the meetings, and when they were over, she studied her Bible some more and was baptized. After her surgery she seemed a little more dedicated for some reason. Before the surgery her commitment was split. Should she stay with her home church? Or go with this new church that was teaching her so much from God's Word?

I asked her if being sick and lying in the hospital helped put everything in perspective.

"No, not really."

"Well, was it the pastor's presentation of God's Word that made you see a clear difference?" I asked.

She shared, "The pastor was nice, and seemed real smart, and did a great job, but to be honest it really wasn't that."

"What exactly was it," I said

"When I was in the hospital, my so-called friends never came to see me. Whenever I would ask for help in understanding the Scriptures, they told me not to worry about little differences. They kept telling me they were my friends, and this church was not the least bit concerned with me. They told me to listen to the ones who care for you. Forget about that stupid church."

She continued, "Yet, when I was in the hospital, and I don't have much family in the area, my so-called friends all knew I was going in for surgery and never came to visit, not once. I did get visits from members of your church, and I have only been attending for a short time. They would sit and talk with me, and the day wasn't so long. I did have time to think. I thought some about the new things I learned in God's Word, and that was good. Mostly I thought about friendship. Who were my friends? The ones who said they were my friends or the ones who showed they were my friends? I now have a great, Bible-based church and great friends. Those visits are what made the difference."

There was another couple who came in through Bible studies that I gave to them. They were comfortable with their church but chose to follow God's Word. They joined the church, but after awhile they became discouraged for one reason or another. They ended up leaving the church and going back to the church they came from.

The mother shared this with me because it was her daughter and son-in-law who left the church. I told her that was too bad. I felt bad for the couple as well as the mother. She told me they had been gone for some time now. She added that no one from our little church or the pastor had gone to see them since they left. That was a real shame. Would a couple of visits from the members or the pastor made the difference? I don't know. What I do know is that it wouldn't have hurt!

Here's something to think about. In a church that believes Christians should be Christ–like, so they try to pattern their lives after Christ. They believe His Word and understand that loving God supremely will change a person. They believe that if we love Christ, we will keep His commandments (John 14:15, 21).

When we change our lives and dedicate them to Christ, sometimes something happens in our social lives. Things we did and once enjoyed, we may not do anymore. I have talked to people who loved alcohol, night clubs, and much more. Those things became unimportant when they began a walk with God. Normally, you don't do those things alone, so your friends might change also. In fact, that happens in almost every case.

It may be much simpler than that. The lady who had surgery lost her friends by simply changing churches. They more or less wrote her off because of her choice. That kind of thing happens all the time. There is nothing or very little we can do about that; it is a fact of life. The question for us is: what is our (the church's) responsibility?

Since we can't keep the new people's friends from losing interest in them, we can be new friends. We should make it a point to interact and befriend new members. Do something with them, talk to them. Find out their interests. Let them know you are there for them. Many times we show interest right up to the time they are baptized, and then we back off.

It isn't intentional; we just figure we have passed that hurdle. They made their decision, they are in the church and we can all rest easy now. The problem is they have most likely lost friends in the process. We need to fill that gap. If a new member doesn't find at least six friends within the first six months of attending a new church, they will almost always leave.

This is why visiting makes such a difference. There is not much point in working to get people in the front door only to watch them leave out the back. We can all visit, and we can all be someone's friend. Even if you can't get out, you can make a phone call. You can send a card or an e-mail. Let someone know that you care, and it will mean a lot more than you can ever imagine.

Chapter 9

The New Pastor Arrives

The time came when the church was informed that the new pastor was available for us to meet and interview. The meeting took place at the larger of the two churches. At that point we were at around thirty members and still growing. We didn't really have any decision on hiring him, so the meeting was more for him than us. If after he talked with the two churches, he had a bad feeling that this would be a poor match, he could decline to take the position.

He asked the typical questions, and we asked the typical questions; then the decision was up to him to become the new pastor. I didn't have anything against him, but I wasn't blown out of the water at the interview either. He answered most of the questions well and conducted himself well.

People asked all kinds of questions and all seemed satisfied. The one question I had on my heart I couldn't ask. It would have been "We have worked very hard to build this little church and have tripled the membership. My question to you is, 'You are not going to come in and mess that up, are you?'" You can see why I couldn't ask that question.

No one wants to see hard work go down the drain. Our growing band had to keep on doing the things that got us to that point. We had to remember that we were the church. If we continued to focus on this then we would be fine. We had to stay positive and receive this new pastor with a warm welcome. We did just that and hoped for the best.

Sometimes something happens that gives a person a good feeling or not such a good feeling. This was one of those times. Just after the pastor arrived, he was met by two relatively new members. I was in the room but wasn't part of the conversation. This couple had a burden to sing and witness to the folks in the local nursing home. She played the guitar and sang and did a good job. He somewhat sang and could share a Bible passage, so they made a good team.

It was news to me, but evidently, this couple had tried to get their program approved for years. Supposedly, she had asked previous pastors to set up a committee to approve it, send the request to the board, and hopefully get permission to do it. That was how the conversation went. So after they finished the conversation they asked the pastor if he would begin the process to get approval.

"No," he said.

That got my attention. I thought, "What is he doing? 'No,' is a little rude."

Then the new pastor added, "Do you really have a burden to reach out to those people through song and God's Word?"

"Yes," they replied, their voices still a little shocked from the "No."

"Then go to the nursing home, tell them about your program. If they give you permission, then do it."

"There is no need for a committee. We can and will approve it if all you're going to do is sing hymns and share God's Word. Get down there, get permission, and put a smile on all those faces."

They smiled and said, "Well okay, but is that all there is to it?"

"Yes," he said, "that's all there is to it."

I was instantly impressed. He cut through all the red tape to get things done. "This guy might just be alright," I thought.

As time went on, I became even more impressed. After he got his feet wet and felt at home with the church members, he and I would go visiting together. Two things were accomplished when we visited; first, the visiting, which he was big on. Second, we had time to talk as we went to and from our visits. These times were important to both of us. We learned about each other and learned from each other. I realized that he had the same concern for souls as I did.

This pastor got along with the people just fine. He had a friendly way, and the people were impressed by that. I was impressed for a different reason. This pastor knew he was there to help. He wasn't there to run the church. He knew someday he would take a call somewhere else and be involved in another church. His attitude was how can I assist you in running your church?

He had another philosophy where we saw eye-to-eye. That was the basic role of the church. One of the first sermons the pastor spoke was on the importance of relationships. He said that our relationship with Christ was more important than anything else. That got my attention.

He went on to say, "If we don't get that right, then everything else we do doesn't really matter."[3]

This began to scare me a little. I have heard some pastors eliminate any responsibilities that God may have for us. Some go on to say all we need is love and nothing else matters. Some believe we are saved in our sins, not from them.

"I know and believe that we are saved by grace through faith, not of our works or good deeds (see Ephesians 2:8). I also know that once we become born-again Christians, we are to walk in the newness of life (see Romans 6:4). A changed person thinks and acts differently. We may and probably will fall, but we have to get back up and follow in the footsteps of Christ," the new pastor continued. "I'm not going to preach a sermon on the balance of faith and works, but there is a balance."

By the end of the sermon, the new pastor got it right. He wasn't preaching that you can work yourself into heaven because you can't. He also wasn't preaching cheap grace. He understood the balance and knew how to present it.

That fit right into my rule number one. Make the church the safest place to go to. This pastor felt if we keep getting more people into the church and they feel safe, if all have an enjoyable experience, then they will want to return and stay. That's

---

[3] Author's paraphrase of the sermon.

where we want them. We certainly can't work with someone who isn't there.

Also, there is a lot of work to do in the church and most churches have a system to put the members to work. There are many offices that need to be filled, for example, elders, deacons, deaconesses, teachers for the adults and children, etc. If you have a sound system, there needs to be qualified people to tend to that. The point is people have to be placed in these positions to have a growing, organized church.

How these positions are filled has a big impact on the growth of a church. Some church pastors and leaders fill these positions in a well, thought-out way that enhances the church growth. Others make decisions in a way that causes problems and impedes church progress.

I have set on committees where they would give an office to a new or unqualified member just to try to make them feel important. The thought might have been good, but the results are usually disastrous for all concerned. This pastor understood that. New members need to feel loved and important, but giving them a responsibility that they are not ready for doesn't work.

There should be a lot of thought and prayer to get the right person for the right job. I wouldn't have an unqualified person manage my construction business just to make them feel good. If I did, I wouldn't have a business for long. The same principle is important for God's church. God's Word explains that we are all given different talents and gifts. Matching the right talent to the right office is very important. Time and prayerful consideration should be exercised to fill all positions big or small.

Christ is our example he taught doctrine. He preached repentance. "Repent, for the kingdom of heaven is at hand" (Matthew 4:17). Yes, He preached, "Keep My commandments" (John 14:15). He did all that, but He did it in love, and so should we. If we reflect the character of Christ, I believe the Holy Spirit will lead them into all truth. My point is that we were on the same page and same focus. We definitely had our differences, but that just allowed us to learn from one another. We believed in unity not uniformity.

Another thing the new pastor did was to tell us that he wanted the church to have three evangelistic series in the next year. I told him, "Wow, that is a lot! You're going to be very busy this year."

"You're right I am."

"When are you going to find time for all that?" I asked.

"Well, I'm starting mine in about six weeks."

"Great!" Then I said, "Wait, what do you mean you are starting 'yours'?"

"Just what I said, 'mine.'"

"Well," I said, "When are you going to start the other two?"

"I'm not," he replied.

"Pastor, you said you were going to have three."

"No," he said, "I said the church is going to have three."

"Who is going to have the other two?"

"You guys," he said with a grin.

"Us guys," I said with no grin. "Us guys, who?"

"You guys, the church," the pastor replied.

Then he reminded me who I had said the church was—the people.

"Yes," I admitted, "I've said that on a number of occasions."

"Well, get busy, get it organized, and if I can help, let me know."

He had his six-week series downtown in a local bank at night. They had a great room they rented for almost nothing. In a few weeks he had some new interests and we had another couple coming to church. My sister and brother-in-law moved to the area, and they had adopted eight children. Just like that we had ten more people. Our total was just over forty.

The church did put on the other two series and the pastor was a lot of help. He told us to present the truth as it is in the Bible, but to do it our way. There were six of us involved in the other two series, and they went well. I think we learned more than the people we were presenting it to.

One day the pastor was speaking on how well the church was growing. He had heard stories of the small band that started it. Most of the growth was before he arrived. He went on to say that the most amazing thing about the growth was that he had nothing to do with it. He said that the church members were responsible for almost all of it.

He said that he was proud of us, and we all felt good. I gained a lot of respect for him that day. Many times people will take the credit but pass the blame. He didn't do this. He recognized what we as a church were all about and worked with us to accomplish our goals.

This pastor wasn't afraid to handle the difficult situations either. Sometimes a situation would come up that had to be addressed. He didn't back down, and he didn't rush in. We would talk about it, get our facts straight, and then deal with the problem.

He didn't have perfect people to work with, but we were focused in the right direction. He made mistakes too, but I could talk to him, and he would listen. If he didn't agree he would tell me. We would talk it out and usually come to some sort of an agreement. There were times when he admitted he didn't handle every situation as well as he could have.

The point is I always felt that my thoughts mattered. The members felt that the church was the people, not the pastor or the building. If you have a pastor with that attitude, I believe that you should consider yourselves lucky. I know that we did.

Chapter 10

Dealing with the Devil

The church members were excited about the growth. Lots of good things were happening. I mentioned some of them; evangelistic meetings, one-on-one Bible studies, group Bible studies, visiting, and much more. Besides all the positive programs, we had a feeling of unity.

That was the good news. All wasn't perfect all the time. We had some challenges also. We had a couple get upset and leave. Despite our efforts, they didn't come back. They didn't tell me the problem; they said they were just making a change. I still have kept in contact with them, but they are happy where they are at.

We had a couple of instances where one or more members would see something that they didn't agree with. It didn't matter if it was a member or visitor. These members felt it was their duty to straighten out the situation right then and there. They would march over to the individual and explain to him or her the evil of his or her ways. One such instance was a visitor who brought a date from a different ethnic background.

The good news is ... well, there was no good news. The couple left and never returned. I talked to the couple and apologized; they understood. I don't even think they were all that mad, but they never came back. I disagreed with the members' thinking on the subject. I think they were wrong. That's not even the point. Even if they were right, it was dead wrong to address it there.

If people want to twist Scripture way out of whack to suit their own prejudice, that's their problem. When we bring it out in the open in church and verbally attack others, then it's everybody's problem. Everybody who wants a warm friendly church that is. Even legitimate problems should be handled with care and tack. Besides, verbally attacking someone in church breaks rule number, and we as a church agreed that that would not be tolerated. Situations like this would motivate me to make a visit and explain, "Thou shalt not break rule number one."

The last I heard, there were more than 3,000 different religions. I don't know what the number is today, but it's a bunch. Some are very similar and some are very different. Even in the same church, there are different understanding of parts of Scripture. There is a different focus on different topics. Some people have just turned their hearts and lives to the Lord today or this week.

Others made the decision years and years ago and have greater understanding. They have had the opportunity to study for a lifetime. If church was a school then you may have grades, kindergarten through college. In church there are no grades; we are all together. We all can feel good about that until someone pushes his or her own opinion down the throats of people until they gag.

Even that wouldn't be so bad except sometimes they make people gag in church in front of everybody. However, we do it all in the name of the Lord. That somehow is supposed to make the gagging pleasant. Well it isn't pleasant; it isn't Christ-like.

In another situation, a lady who had recently joined the church wanted to reach out at Christmastime to her new Christian friends. She decided to have a women's baking party at one of the homes. A warm invitation was sent out to all the women so no one would be left out. Many decided to go and had a great time. The new member was excited with most of the responses. However, one response caused hurt and confusion.

The new member did receive a letter that, in her opinion, told her she was a pagan. The letter explained that Christmas is a pagan holiday not Christ's birthday. In the concerned letter-writer's opinion, baking holiday cookies was not only unhealthy but also a pagan practice. The new lady didn't understand what was so wrong with what she did. I am not new, and I don't understand what she did wrong either.

I believe a nice letter saying, "Thanks for the invitation, but I will not be able to attend" would have been a lot better. A letter like the one she received didn't help; the result was hurt and a feeling of rejection. I know hurt and rejection wasn't the intention; it was just the logical result of a letter like that. I saw the letter. I really believe it was sent with useful information in mind. It wasn't sent by an evil person who hated the one it was sent to. I believe there was little or no thought put into the possible downside to a letter like this.

Another point is, how do we spend our time? The letter-writer had weeks' worth of opportunity to be a friend to this new lady. She could have spent a little time getting to know her. That didn't happen. Why wasn't time and effort spent being a friend and building a relationship? Maybe there just wasn't time. I don't know. What I do know is time was found, and effort was taken, to sit down and compose this hurtful letter.

There is a saying that it is the unloaded gun that kills people. Someone has an unloaded gun; he wants to have fun. The gun is pointed at a friend, thinking it will scare him, and then both of them will have a big laugh. The trigger is pulled. Instead of a harmless "click," there is a deadly BANG! That noise will never go away, and the friend slumps to the ground. Instead of fun and laughter, there is silence and death.

"I thought the gun was unloaded," the stunned killer exclaims.

Our words, letters, seemingly harmless gossip, may be anything but harmless. Our words can be very dangerous or very helpful. Be sure you understand what you're shooting at. Be sure you understand the possible result of your message. Count the cost before you pull that trigger. Is it worth it?

The wisest man who ever lived wrote, "Death and life are in the power of the tongue" (Proverbs 18:21). Words have killed people. Suicides have been committed by an uncontrolled tongue. Consider your words carefully, Christian.

Why do I write these stories? It is not to expose anyone; that wouldn't do any good. In fact, I wouldn't tell who these individuals were if I were asked. These are examples of what happens or what will happen in most if not all churches. You and I may even take part in a similar situation. We may be the hurt one. We may be the ones doing the hurting. I hope that's not the case.

The point is this kind of thing happens. How do we deal with it as a person? How do we deal with it as a church? Let's get the blame and origin right. When someone causes needless pain, the devil is behind it. When someone lies and says bad things about you or anyone else, the devil is behind it. The devil wants to rip God's people apart. In many cases he has done a pretty good job of it.

First Peter 5:8 tells us: "The devil walks about like a roaring lion, seeking whom he may devour." The devil wants God's work to cease. The devil wants to destroy or devour God's people. When a lion roars, many times that paralyzes its victim. A church may be going along well, making great progress, and then a member roars. The result is paralyzing at times. It may surprise you to know that a hurtful whisper may come out as a roar.

As members, we have to continually pray and soul-search. We would do well to have the attitude of the disciples when told "one of you will betray Me." Matthew 26:21, 22 makes the point. At the last supper Jesus made the statement: "Assuredly, I say to you, one of you will betray me" (verse 21). The disciples with a sad hearts asked "Lord, is it I?" (verse 22).

Most of the time when a difficult situation comes up, without thinking, we exclaim it's not me. It's human nature to respond like that. Maybe it would be better to think before we speak. Then if there could be any involvement at all on our part, we would ask, "Is it I?" Did I have anything to do with it at all? If you did, give the offended person a heartfelt apology. That would go a long way toward shutting up the beast.

If more members would do this, we would have churches bursting at the seams. The problem is far too few take ownership of their shortcomings. My church and your church probably will not change that because some things have to be changed as individuals. We have just mentioned what to do "as a member." What does the church do with those who say hurtful things to people? There are those who will come up with all sorts of answers. Those answers may range from doing nothing to hanging them from the steeple of the church.

The sad reality is there is very little the church can do to stop people from being hurtful. We can try to explain that their actions are hurtful and hope they change. Many times those who are hurting others believe that God is leading them. This isn't a new problem.

John 8:40–44 tells of Jewish leaders who claimed God as their Father (verse 41). These same people were trying to kill the Son of God. Jesus told them "You are of your father the devil" (verse 44). In context Jesus told them that God's children don't act like you. The devil's children act exactly like you, that is why you are the devil's children. The point is that Jesus didn't change them from hurting people and neither will we.

I said the church members can do very little to change hurtful people. However, that doesn't mean we are to do very little. It means we are to focus on where we can do something. Throughout the Bible we are told to be kind to those we meet. Christ is our example and he was sent "to heal the brokenhearted" (Luke 4:18). When someone has been hurt, heal them or at least comfort them. Tell them that they have been a target of the devil. "Heal the brokenhearted."

Tell them they are loved and don't worry about the "tares."[4] In God's church both will grow together. God has promised that. He has also promised He will take care of the tare problem. Those weedy people were placed there by the enemy (see Matthew 13:25). Those causing heartache and pain, we are told if they don't change and they remain tares, will be put in bundles and burned (Matthew 13:30).

---

[4] The parable of the wheat and the tares is found in Matthew 13:24–30.

If you have been hurt and someone reaches out to you, usually you feel a little better. Imagine if half the church reached out to you. Get together as a church and show those who are hurting that the wheat outnumbers the tares.

When we see how the devil has such a negative effect on others, there is something we should do. Pray that we don't act like that. Matthew 26 talks about when Christ was about to go through those finale hours, He knew the disciples would be tempted by the devil. Christ told the disciples to watch and pray. They fell asleep instead.

Christ told the disciples they would be made to stumble, or give in to the devil. Peter said the others might stumble or be convinced by the devil to leave, but he wouldn't. (I'm paraphrasing but read the account in Matthew 26.) Peter was so sure he would never be tempted of the devil. That confidence, with the lack of watching and praying, made him an easy target for the devil.

Watching and praying and studying God's Word is how we deal with the devil. James 4:7, 8 says, "Therefore submit to God. Resist the devil and he will flee from you. Draw near to God and He will draw near to you. Cleanse your hands, you sinners; and purify your hearts, you double-minded."

We deal with the devil by praying that the Lord will strengthen us, just like Christ prayed for strength. We need to do the works of Christ that will draw us to Him. The difference between doing what God wants or what we want is many times a matter of submitting. "Not as I will, but as You will" (Matthew 26:39). These words of our Savior are words of example to us. Our confidence needs to be in Christ, not ourselves. Our focus needs to be on others. When we feel slighted or hurt, think of the hurt the cross caused. Christ gave everything for us; let's give something back.

Chapter 11

Time for a Rest

I would like to create a picture in your mind. Maybe this doesn't apply to you. Maybe none of the following has ever been the case. If that's true, then praise God. Even if this doesn't apply to you, it does to some, including me at times. So try to get a picture in your mind.

Sometimes life is just plain difficult. Sometimes a week flies by, and I feel just as great at the end as I did when it started. That is seldom the case. Sometimes I have literally prayed, "TGIF"—thank God it's Friday. I have had weeks I couldn't wait until they ended. There were problems at work whether it be a co-worker or just the stress of the job itself.

Responsibilities pile up, like dealing with the family, paying bills, and a host of other concerns. Yes, for me life can be overwhelming at times. Sometimes our problems are self-inflicted and sometimes not. The one thing they both have in common is that they are still problems. As I have talked and visited with many others, I have decided I am not alone.

Like many others I get up every morning like a warrior going into battle. I put on my armor and grab my sword so that I am ready for whatever may come my way. We have to be on our guard so we don't get blindsided. It has been said that "a good defense is a strong offense." Don't look for trouble, but be prepared if it comes.

Today will be different. Your weapons will be different. I am a construction worker. My weapons would be a hammer, saw, nail bag, etc. A doctor's would be a stethoscope; a cook would use pots and pans. We all have our weapons. Today, however, the weapons have changed. Today is a day to lay down your armor. Today is the day we should get up with a different attitude, a different state of mind.

Today, we will not be going to work, we are going to church. I hope we still have a weapon, but it will be a different weapon; today's weapon will be the Word of God. For one day we can forget the stress of the world, the everyday grind. Everyday problems can wait for twenty-four hours.

We know our bills won't go away. We know life goes on. Today, however, is a new day. We have something else to concentrate on, something better to focus our energy on. Today is a day to rejoice and remember.

In the heart of God's Ten Commandments, God said, "Remember." "Remember the Sabbath day, to keep it holy" (Exodus 20:8). The command goes on to say that work should be put aside. It is God's day; let's keep it that way. What a relief! For most of the world we as Christians are free to go to church and enjoy a wonderful day, worshipping God, singing praises to His name, and feeling the love and support from our fellow Christian brothers and sisters.

This day of rest couldn't have come at a better time. Our batteries need recharging as they get really low. Church will be a perfect place for this to happen. Not only our batteries, but also our energy is usually low. Maybe our bubbly personality and great attitudes were in the danger zone as well. That's alright because now we are in church.

Christ understands that some of us have had a hard week. He understands that we may be hanging by a thread. He gives us a solution in His Word. "Come unto me, all ye that labor and are heavy laden, and I will give you rest" (Matthew 11:28 KJV). That is a wonderful promise. It is great to have a Savior who really understands us and provides a haven of rest. He recognizes our every need. Today will be great.

So armed with the Word of God and a good feeling in our hearts, we are off to church. What could possibly go wrong? God has a day for church, His people will be there, and I have absolutely nothing to worry about. I hope I have painted a mental picture in your mind that should take place every time we go to church.

It's like a painting of a big, happy family enjoying Christmas or Thanksgiving dinner together. All the family members are laughing and having a great time. You and I know that every family isn't like that, although it may be that way in pictures. In real life some families have anything but total bliss and happiness.

Unfortunately, not all churches are in perfect harmony either. Some churches have people fighting for control. Some churches have cliques or small groups that no others are allowed to penetrate. The outsiders are encouraged to find their own groups. Some have people who are looking so hard for their own group that they look right over you. Many churches have some, if not all, of these situations in their church every week.

When these things exist, we wish we had our everyday armor back. We feel beaten and bruised. We go home with more stress instead of less. Somehow our "day of rest" turned into a "day of stress." All in all, we can't wait to get home. We felt much better before church than after.

I heard a true story awhile back of a person who was trying to witness to a lady who appeared to be down on her luck. This lady was asked how everything was going, and she said that she had some health problems and personal problems, describing several. The lady added that she really didn't have any friends anymore. The person witnessing was at a loss as to how to help her, but she did finally come up with an idea.

"Would you like to come to church this week?" the helper asked.

"Church!" exclaimed the lady "No, I would not like to go to church. Haven't you been listening to me and my problems?"

"Yes," the helper said, "I have been listening.

"Well," the lady said, "I feel bad enough already. What would I want to go to church for? I can get talked about anytime. I certainly don't have to go to church for it."

What all the circumstances were, I never knew. Why she was so bitter was probably due to one or maybe several bad experiences in some church. The one common denominator in someone being hurt at church is, in almost every case, rule number one was not top priority—"Make the church the safest, most enjoyable place to go."

It is true that I didn't know any of the circumstances in the discouraged lady's case. There is one case I did know something about. A good friend of mine who I have known for many years wrote me a letter recently. She is not only a good friend but also a strong influence in her church. As far as I knew, she was always involved and excited about her church.

She has been active in Bible studies, evangelistic meetings, and has been responsible for leading others to Christ. Besides that, she and her husband had gone on several mission trips. Not only has this couple donated their time but also their finances. In general they have both exercised self-sacrifice to further the work of God.

Now back to her letter: to my surprise she wasn't always excited about her church. In her letter she shared that she was raised by Christian parents, went to the Christian schools, married, and her children went to church and church school as well. Then at one point she became disinterested in church and stopped going.

She did go once in a while but was no longer a regular member. Several years passed, and she thought that she would go back to church. She was living in Florida at the time, so she went to the same denomination she was brought up in.

"No one even noticed that I was there. I was a stranger when I walked in, and a stranger when I walked out," she said. "No one asked me where I was from, how long I would be there, or anything. In fact, no one even spoke to me, except the so-called greeter. A short 'hello' was all I got. I went back a couple of times and always was received the same."

After a few weeks of that, I think she remembered why she left the church in the first place. Those are my words, not hers.

The result was to stay home or do something that was exciting or pleasant. Church certainly wasn't either of those.

She then moved from Florida to the Carolinas. Again, she decided to visit a church once she was settled. It is funny how sometimes the conscience or something just keeps pestering a person to get back on track. "Train up a child in the way he should go, and when he is old he will not depart from it" (Proverbs 22:6).

These are words of encouragement for anyone with friends or family who have left the church. We may ask ourselves when we have been kind to someone, represented the character of Christ the best we could, and gave him or her the best spiritual shot we possibly could, why did he or she leave anyway? Oftentimes we don't know "the rest of the story." Sometimes we leave a seed that will spring up years later. Christ never leaves us or forsakes us (see Hebrews 13:5). We should never lose hope and never quit praying for the Spirit of Christ to lead them back.

On with her story: "I moved to the Carolinas, and God placed two angels at the entrance to the church. They weren't really angels, but those two ladies gave me the best welcome I ever had. They were a breath of fresh air. I wanted to go back just to see those two ladies.

"If I missed a week, I got a card saying I was missed. Besides the card, my husband and I would get a visit. They were truly interested in me. That was a time in my life when I needed that. I can't tell you how much that meant. It just meant everything.

"My mother visited with me for a while, and I saw her talking to the pastor. I could overhear her saying to him, 'Pastor, you need to visit my daughter. She has just started to come back to church and could use a visit.' You have to love a mother even when she is meddling. I have come to realize that is what a loving mother does best sometimes.

"Even though my mother strongly advised the pastor to visit me, he never did. I was a little disappointed, but the two ladies never let me down. I really don't think I would have returned to that church if it wasn't for those two women.

"As it turned out, those ladies never quit making me and others feel welcome. I found my way back to the church and have been there ever since. I have never forgotten that warmth and kindness and the change it made in my life. I made some bad decisions, and it was nobody's fault but my own that I left. I blame myself for that, but praise God for the two angels he sent as greeters."

I have met those two ladies and never knew that story. I did know that they were very kind and made anyone feel comfortable around them immediately. I don't know what formal training they had. I would imagine that they didn't have any. They knew their Bible enough to share a word of comfort when needed. They knew what they believed and could back it up with God's Word.

My friend didn't need a theologian or a Bible scholar. She didn't need a Bible study, even though the women were more than capable of that. As I said earlier, I don't know what knowledge or formal training if any they had. What I do know for sure is that both of those ladies knew and understood rule number one.

My friend finished her letter by telling me about her daughter in Michigan. "My daughter has been going to a church in Michigan. When she first started going, some of the church members were very friendly. However, the pastor's wife has never said two words to her.

"When my daughter said 'good morning,' the pastor's wife just sorta nodded. She doesn't feel comfortable around her now."

Thank God for the kind members who kept her interest and kept her going back to church. I have met her daughter briefly a couple of times. I don't know a lot about her. I do know that she is very outgoing. She is one of those people who make you feel that you have known her for a long time from the first time you meet. I believe she is what I call "high octane." She is friendly and would respond positively to friendliness. I would hope she feels comfortable and at home in her church.

Sometimes when newcomers arrive in a church, several people go out of their way to make them feel welcome. That is great. Then sometimes, after a short while, it slows down. The welcome committee feels they have done their job and reverts back to their circle of friends they are use to. This is natural, but in many cases very dangerous.

Remember, making your church the safest, most enjoyable place, or rule number one, has no expiration date. Instead of backing off the relationship you started, you should be getting others involved to befriend them.

Chapter 12

Power of Choice

By now I'm sure you understand rule number one. Do your part to make your church the safest, most enjoyable church to go to. There is so much more to church than that. Church is progressive. Spiritually, we are always learning and growing. It doesn't matter if we have started a relationship with Christ sixty minutes ago or sixty years ago. We are always supposed to be growing in Christ.

Church is not to be considered just a social club. In the Old Testament times, God told Moses to make Him a sanctuary. God also gave the reason: "let them make Me a sanctuary, that I may dwell among them" (Exodus 25:8). God goes to church to. He wants to dwell or be with us.

Christ said in the New Testament: "for where two or three are gathered together in My name, I am there in the midst of them" (Matthew 18:20). Church is a place to study the Scriptures together in Christian fellowship. Those Scriptures have a purpose. Second Timothy 3:15–17 tells us the "Holy Scriptures, which are able to make you wise unto salvation [is] … profitable for doctrine, for reproof, for correction, for instruction in righteousness, that the man of God may be complete, thoroughly equipped for every good work."

We are saved by grace through faith, but the love of God will produce a change in our lives. We will become fishers of men, workers for the cause of Christ. We will be part of the family of

God, and He will teach us. Yes there is much more to do than go to church, sit in the pew with a holy grin on our faces, and do nothing.

Rule number one is important because if we are excited about going to church, we will tend to learn more. Happy people learn much faster. Being kind is showing the love of God. We have a responsibility to treat people as we would want them to treat us (see Matthew 7:12). What happens when that doesn't happen? What happens when we are treated badly? We get angry, we have a bad day, we leave the church, and we feed off the negative words and atmosphere. We forget why we are in church in the first place.

We have talked about the irresponsible behavior and the pain, the hurt, and the stress it causes. What I would like to touch on now is the responsibility of the hurt one. What responsibility does the target of such devastating behavior have? Many times we don't think of the victim's responsibility. We may be completely innocent of wrongdoing; in other words we gave no one any reason to treat us that way.

Is there a responsibility on our part? Think of our reaction, for example, if someone is saying cruel things to us or about us. How do we react? Many times I have seen people get angry, react like the aggressor in retaliation, or even leave the church and the faith. These are devastating reactions for both the person and for the church.

When a person says something to someone, and that person gets upset and leaves the church that is powerful. There is strength in a person who can cause someone's faith to be shattered by just a conversation. Where does one get strength like that? Some may say the devil. Indirectly, that may be true.

If you have been a target of someone's verbal assault, and the attack is powerful enough to make you have a bad reaction, then the enemy's power came from you. Before you throw this book down and think I'm crazy, let me explain. Treating you badly was a choice on their part. True it was a bad choice, but it was a choice. How that affects you is not their choice, it is your choice.

For example, if someone told you they didn't like you because you were Abraham Lincoln, you most likely wouldn't be mad because for starters you're not Abraham Lincoln. If the same person called you a stupid idiot, you may have a bad reaction. You may not be any more of an idiot than you are Abraham Lincoln. So why the bad reaction?

If we react like someone wants us to, we have given them power. If we don't, we totally take that power away. When the reaction is kind or even ignored, their power is gone. In fact, many times they will get angry when there is no reaction. Who has the power now?

I was driving down the road with a friend who I was giving Bible studies to. Someone passed us and gestured in a terrible way. We were both young and aggressive, and my first thought was in anger to run him down to explain our displeasure. We were both capable of doing that.

Then we decided that driver's evil conduct was not going to dictate who we were and how we would feel. That really felt good. I have been the type of person that when pushed to push back. If someone disrespected me that way, I used to be upset for some time.

Not that time, in a matter of seconds we were both back laughing and enjoying the day and discussing God's Word. That time I used my power of choice wisely. We learned a little lesson that day. We can't help what someone does all the time, but we always have a choice. Has that system always worked for me all the time? Sadly, no. That doesn't change the fact that I always had a choice.

This too is a process. It is a growing experience. Once you try it a couple of times, and have victory, you begin to see the wisdom. In my case it gave me one more thing to pray about. I pray for a calm and kind spirit, and in my life it has made a difference.

This "turn the other cheek" principle is a biblical principle (see Matthew 5:39). More than that let's look at another scenario. You may have to use your imagination a little. We all know that little things turn into big things. Married couples have been at each others' throats and when they finally analyzed the reason they were fighting, they were shocked at their childish behavior. I have heard it said many times "That was such a stupid argument."

Back to the scenario: you get ready for church, put on the dress you have picked out, grab your Bible, and off to church you go. You're feeling pretty good, and you are enjoying the day at church. Then one of the self-appointed saints is looking your way but talking to another pillar of the church. They are old and maybe a little hard of hearing, so they talk louder than they realize.

Then it happens. You hear one of them say, "That dress looks like it belongs in a saloon not in church, who does she thinks she is anyway?"

The other lady replies, "Well, I think she comes here for all the wrong reasons anyway. If she can't keep her mind out of the gutter, she should just stay home."

You're instantly hurt and offended. You go through the rest of the service in disbelief. You don't even know what the sermon was about. The ride home is painful, and you just want to get those words out of your head. The words not only stay but are played over and over. It is not just the words but the disgusting look they gave you.

You can see them talking about you even when you close your eyes. After the hurt comes anger.

"Who do I think I am?" you say in your mind, "Who do they think they are?"

The week goes on and some days you hardly think of it, some you do. Then comes the week end, and it's time to go to church. The situation comes back to your mind clear as a bell.

You decide this week you have better things to do this week. You will just hang out with a friend. You call her up, she visits you, and the two of you talk.

"Why aren't you in church?" your friend asks.

You tell them the whole sordid story. The more you talk, the angrier you get.

"Church people are just a bunch of hypocrites anyway," your friend replies.

In your state of mind you agree. Next week you do the same thing. Pretty soon you're not really that mad, but you're just not in the mood anymore. You have made a decision to forget this church stuff and go on with your life. Sure, this is just a made up story, but I have heard too many real ones that sound just about like that.

The two ladies made a decision to break rule number one. They chose to gossip, making the church a hurtful place to be. They were rude and uncaring, and there is no excuse for that. Here is something to think about. What choice did the victim have in what the two ladies did? The answer is "no choice."

What choice did the victim have on how those two ladies affected her? The answer is "plenty." Sometimes when you are blindsided by an uncaring and thoughtless remark, you just react. That's human, but at some point you need to start thinking and the sooner the better.

If you don't, you could give someone power to ruin your day. Then give them power to ruin your week. Then give them power to keep you from going to church. What's next? Are you going to give them power to keep you out of God's kingdom also? That's a whole lot of power to give away. It is sure worth thinking about, isn't it?

Can you imagine not making eternity with Christ? He asks you: "Why?"

You say, "Well, these ladies were mean and hurt my feelings."

He looks at you with sad eyes and says, "I wanted you to be with Me for eternity. I had people call Me names like blasphemer, Beelzebub, the devil, and many more. I was beaten, my beard pulled out, slugged in the face, and nailed to a cross. Then I was killed, all for you. Would it really have been that hard to ignore those two women for Me?"

I am not making light of the terrible things that people do, and doing those things in the church is beyond irresponsible. I have seen friends who I have studied with for years get mad and leave over some ridiculous behavior. Sometimes this terrible behavior has come from pastors or church leaders. The devil knows how the game is played and he plays it well.

If we expect to get a church off life-support and make it healthy again, we need to be tough. One day I met an old gentleman who had worked in the church all his life. I was discouraged because I was pouring my heart into building up a church. Some of the people were very receptive and supportive. Some, however, were not; they were rude and seemed to work against everything I was trying to do.

Anyway, this gentleman came over and told me I was doing a good work. I should have been encouraged but was not. He tried a little harder to cheer me up, but I wasn't in the mood for cheer.

Then he said, "I am going to tell you something, son. If you are going to be serious about working for God, you need to have armadillo skin.

"Do you know what an armadillo is?"

"Yes," I said, "it's a big rat with a hard shell."

"Close enough. The point is, son, if you don't have thick skin, you may as well get out now. The devil will throw everything he has at God's people. It will take a strong faith and thick skin."

I smiled a little and understood that he was right.

An old preacher was talking one day, and I was pretty interested. This is when I was quite young and didn't listen to well to sermons. This one, however, got my attention. Part way through the sermon the pastor quoted a nursery rhyme.

> Pussy cat, pussy cat, where have you been?

> I've been down to London to visit the Queen.

> Pussy cat, pussy cat, what did you do there?

> I frightened a little mouse, under the chair.

Then this old pastor shared that he had been to London. He had seen the crown jewels. He had saw Buckingham palace and the changing of the guard. He had seen a lot of wonderful and exciting things. Yet the cat went to London, and all the cat saw was a mouse. All the cat did while in London was chase that mouse under the chair.

"Why did the cat do that in London?" the preacher asked. "Because that is what a cat looks for, and that is what a cat wants to do is chase mice. You and I have the freedom to go to church. We have already read the text that tells us 'For where two or three are gathered together in My name, I am there in the midst of them'" (Matthew 18:20).

That old pastor's point was clear: Christ is in our churches. If we are looking and searching for Him, we will find him. If we are looking for those who the devil has planted to discourage us, we will find them to. Why are we really going to church? Who are we really trying to see? Are we going to feel Christ's presence and fellowship with the saints in His church? Or are we going to get distracted by the mouse under the chair? I believe with all my heart it's a matter of choice, our choice.

Chapter 13

Send Them Away!

Jesus spent his time on earth helping and healing others, which is what drew people to Him. The disciples were also moved by the depth and love of Jesus. They were impressed with the tenderness and compassion that Jesus showed every day. They had to be proud of such a kindhearted leader. They were, well, most of the time.

There were times when Jesus was too compassionate for His own good. There were times when Jesus wasted His precious time and effort. Not only that, He wasted the disciples precious time and effort. Many times Jesus could have accomplished more if He didn't get sidetracked on lost causes. Being loving and kind was great up to a point but at times Jesus took it a little too far. Or so the disciples thought.

At the end of Matthew 14, we can read where Jesus healed many. In fact, many were healed just by touching His garment (see Matthew 14:36). Jesus then started to teach a large number of people called a multitude (see Matthew 15:10). This was extremely impressive to the disciples. This is what they wanted and longed for.

Jesus became so popular that huge crowds began to follow Him. This is what it is all about. Impressing just one, two, or the small groups were for the birds. Jesus and the disciples were on their way to stardom. When Jesus talked, the crowds looked like a sea of people. The support was overwhelming.

Then in Matthew 15:21 Jesus did something a little crazy. He took a journey of around fifty to seventy miles on foot, which would take Him at least a week. If I were one of the disciples, I would have thought that this must have been very important. He left the crowds and the thousands of supporters. "I wonder what great thing He is up to now," they each must have thought.

Jesus finally arrived at a "region of Tyre and Sidon." (Matt 15:21) When He got there, a woman cried out to Jesus for help. "Have mercy on me, O Lord, Son of David! My daughter is severely demon-possessed" (Matthew 15:22). The disciples saw this poor woman with her heart broken for her daughter as she pled for help.

They had seen Jesus cast out demons by just a word. Or with simply a touch, the demons would flee. You would think they would have been all excited about Jesus restoring this crazed daughter back to her mother in perfect health. You would think they would have anticipated a miracle born out of compassion.

Not exactly, instead, they advised Jesus on the proper thing to do in a situation like that. "His disciples came and urged Him saying, 'Send her away, for she cries out after us'" (Matthew 15:23). This lady was a "woman from Canaan." They (people of Canaan) worshipped idols and were considered heathen. This woman was different in the eyes of the disciples.

This woman didn't deserve the time of day in their opinion. She certainly didn't deserve the blessings of a Savior. They were disappointed that Jesus even tolerated a person like her near Him. That's why they urged Him to send her away. She was a problem. She was annoying and a troublemaker. They would be much better off if she would just leave.

Jesus pretended to act like the disciples to show them what they were like. Then she shows incredible faith, and her faith was rewarded. Jesus said, "Great is your faith! Let it be to you as you desire." And her daughter was healed from that very hour" (Matthew 15:28).

Jesus had many followers. The disciples would be the leaders of the early church that Jesus was starting. The leadership answer to the problem of a heartbroken woman was "send her away." Many times someone comes into our church that is a little different. They may not be polished enough. They may be too polished for our liking.

They may not dress like us. They may not think like us. They may be annoying with their cries for help. Sometimes the loudest cries are silent. We really don't know what to do with them, so we say send them away. Not in so many words, but our actions are screaming out the message in many cases.

It would be bad enough if it just came from our rough or new church members. Sadly enough it comes from the top at times. The leadership may be trying to run a particular course, and then someone has different ideas. Someone isn't fitting into their plan. Someone is seemingly taking a different path than the one we just laid out for them. "Send them away." "Send them away!" "We will be better off without them."

I have to say at this time we need leadership. We need a course. We need a plan. God's Word talks about a path. Actually, God's Word talks of two. One leads to life eternal, and the other leads to destruction (see Matthew 7:13, 14). We as leaders have to believe in a path. We have to believe in right and wrong. We have to desire to lead others to that path. It is our Christian duty.

In the story of Christ healing the woman's daughter, this woman was a heathen. She most likely worshiped idols. She probably wasn't dressed like your typical God-fearing woman.

Could the disciples change her thinking on idol worship by sending her away? Would this woman be brought to love and understand Jesus as the Messiah by sending her away? Would her daughter, other friends, or family members ever be brought to Christ by sending them away? I think not.

Some among us don't fit in. They are different. They may even be annoying at times. We as God's people should have standards. It seems to me that sending them away by our words or actions is the wrong course. Lovingly accepting them, taking time to know them, and showing them what great things God has done for all of us are the ways to make a difference. Lead those to Christ;

He will change them. Work with them, and show them the two paths. Pray that they follow the one that leads to Christ.

This "send them away" theory is not an isolated case. Jesus was speaking and healing the sick to a great crowd who was following Him. There were 5,000 men, not counting women and children. This crowd has been estimated to have been close to 20,000 counting all. The point is He had been ministering to their needs—their physical needs by healing and their spiritual needs by preaching.

It was getting late and the people were hungry. This was before fast cars and fast food. They needed food to make the journey back home. The disciples knew the situation, but they didn't know what to do about it. What they did know was they didn't want it to be their problem.

They got together and told Jesus to execute their fine plan. They told Jesus "This is a deserted place, and the hour is already late. Send the multitudes away, that they may go into the villages and buy themselves food" (Matthew 14:15). Jesus told them, "You give them something to eat" (Matthew 14:16).

The disciples didn't know what to do, so Jesus took five loaves and two fish, and then He performed a great miracle. All had plenty to eat with some left over. By this time the disciples had seen Jesus work miracles. They themselves had been sent out and performed miracles. They had been empowered to "heal the sick, cleanse the lepers, raise the dead, [and] cast out demons" (Matthew 10:8).

They should have been more concerned about the problem. If their concern was the people instead of themselves, they might have come up with "Plan B." They didn't even ask Jesus what His thoughts were. They didn't say Jesus, "What we can do to help this situation?" The church leaders once again said "send them away." They wanted the problem to go away and at this time the people were the problem.

This Bible passage reminds me of another growth spurt in our little church. Our little group of eight or so when we had started out had grown to about thirty-five. I got a phone call from a good friend at the large church I left to build up this little church. He asked me if I would like to go out to dinner with him. I said I would and we set a time.

I knew this wasn't just a normal invite because we didn't really go out to eat with each other. We would hang out at each other's house or at church but not so much to eat dinner. We met and caught up on all the normal "how are you, etc." Then he said, "I have a little problem."

"What's that?" I asked.

"Well," he said, "There are a few of us men who have gotten together and formed a small study group once a week at the church."

"Great," I said, "What are you studying?"

"We study the Bible and look deeper into the meanings," he explained, "the Ten Commandments are general, but their meanings are much deeper."

"I totally agree. Christ said the same thing when He said that if you kill, you break the law of God. If you hate your brother, you break the same law" (see Matthew 5:21–26).

"That's right," my friend said, "Those are the things we are studying."

He went on to say that they were also doing things in the community.

"Like what?" I asked.

"Helpful services for humanity; for example, a man was confined to a wheelchair and needed a cement path from his house to the mailbox. He couldn't afford it, so our men's group took an afternoon and put it in for him. We believe that helping is a great way to spread the good news of God's Word. Our ultimate goal is that these activities will lead others to Christ."

"Wonderful," I said. "So what's your little problem.'"

"The problem is there are some in our church who think we are trying to work against the church. We are not," he stammered, "We are just trying to do our part as workers for Christ. We would also like it to grow beyond our church similar to the Promise Keepers, that men's group that went nationwide. We are not interfering with the church at all."

"Have you talked to the pastor about it?"

"Yes, and that's the other little problem. He thinks it would be a good idea not to do the program, not to rock the boat. He more or less agrees with the few members that for some reason have a problem with it."

"Well," I said, "I still don't see a big problem. Study at the church once a week like you want, and do your community service when you can. Just don't do the outside work in the church's name so there aren't any legal problems if someone gets hurt."

"We are, but the pastor doesn't want us to meet at the church to study the Bible either."

"Oh, I see the problem. Let me see what I can do," I told him.

I was, and still am, a friend of the pastor, so I thought I would talk to him and get it all worked out. I did meet with him, but his side was slightly different but not much. The bottom line was the church wasn't comfortable in letting those members study there. They had a board meeting and that was that. The board said that there was to be no more studying at the church for those members.

I met with my friend, and he asked, "Well, did you smooth everything over?"

"Not exactly," I said.

"What does that mean?"

"It means you can't study there without a problem. I do have a solution though."

"What's that?"

"Just come over to our church once a week and study the Bible. I just have one stipulation."

"What's that?"

"Just open it up for anybody in our church to study with you."

He smiled and said, "No problem."

The group of five did study at my church. Most of them also moved their memberships to our little church. The point to this experience of mine is this: when the disciples saw a problem, their answer was "send them away." Christ had another answer: "They do not need to go away. You give them something to eat" (Matthew 14:16).

In this story it doesn't matter to me who was right or wrong. The point is there are always going to be people who have the "send them away" attitude. They don't belong. They are trouble. They are not like us. "Send them away." Then there will be those who will heed the Savior's words: "They do not need to go away. You give them something to eat." Which one will you be? If you follow rule number one, you will be in the catering business.

Chapter 14

Six to Sixty

That last story produced close to a dozen new members. The study group was not only no problem, but they also became effective workers in the church. There are always going to be problems as pastors are not angels. At least the ones who I know aren't. They are typically dedicated people with strengths and weaknesses like everybody else.

The church isn't the pastor; it's the people. In Bible times the church or the children of Israel would have a spiritual leader. If the leader was good, the spirituality of the church would be elevated, and the church would prosper. When they had a bad leader, the spirituality would go downhill, and the church would suffer.

The same is true today. The problem back then was the people would tend to follow their leader whether the leader was right or not. Today, some churches have the same problem. Respect your pastor. Help him in his responsibilities when you can, but don't forget it is your church. Your spiritual leader is Christ. That's why you call yourself a Christian.

The church isn't the military. That's why rule number one is so important. The military has never pretended to be the most enjoyable place to be. The military has never portrayed, "Whatever your problems are, we will be patient and kind." That isn't how the military works. When you're in the service, you are their property. You have to do what you're told.

Not in a church, that doesn't work there. You can't have an "Attila the Hun" attitude. The barbarian personality has no place there. You have to have the skills to make the members want to work together, not have to. Their leader needs to be Christ and motivated by the Holy Spirit or interest will be lost, and your church will be back on life support.

In many ways the church is like a business. You have expenses, and you need good organization. Bills have to be paid on time. Things have to have maintenance, doors have to be kept closed, etc. Many things make church like a business. Yet, a lot of things are different. For example, most churches pay their pastors, but the other workers usually do not get paid. There are some exceptions, but that's how it is with most churches.

At work or a business where you get paid, you are expected to produce for that wage. Church is different. At church it is the love for Christ and the love for one another. It's the desire to finish the work, so we can all go home. It's the desire to have Christian fellowship. There are many more Christ-like reasons for going to church, but those are a few examples.

I hope the point is clear. The church needs to be a haven of rest. In the world during the week we get beat up on more than we would like. We certainly don't have to go to church for that. We shouldn't expect all loving messages because sometimes we need to be woken up. Sometimes we need our toes stepped on so we can put them on the right path.

Even these messages are to be done in love. The way Christ would have presented them. Remember the goal is eternity with Christ. Christ preached repent; in other words, change your course. Then he gave the reason: the kingdom of heaven is at hand. He pleads for us to get off the wrong path and find the right path that leads to eternal life.

The story about the woman at the well shows the tenderness of a loving Savior. She had some issues that needed changing. Christ was there to save, not scold. The disciples had written her off as a disgusting human being. Christ saw a precious soul who needed some direction. She evangelized much of a city while the disciples wallowed in their prejudice. They both needed and received a loving lesson that day.

Do you want to see your church grow? Go to church with the spirit of Christ. Go to church with a purpose. That purpose is to seek out someone and make their day at church just a little better. Look for the good in them; it's there if you look.

Do you want your church off life support and flourishing? Then study the fruits of the spirit in Galatians 5:22 and 23. They are love, joy, peace, longsuffering, kindness, goodness, faithfulness, gentleness, and self control. Pray that you will receive these fruits.

When God answers your prayer, and you receive these gifts, take them to church with you. Believe me they will come in handy. Share these gifts with others. Let people know that you are interested in where they are going, not where they have been.

There will be much more success if by your Christ-like example they see where they need to make changes in their lives than if you tell them the evil of their ways. Let them know that we all have sinned and fallen short of what we should be (see Romans 3:23). That's not a license to sin, but an encouragement that we are all in the same boat and need to learn and work together.

Lead all you can to the foot of the cross and the feet of Jesus. Let Christ and the Holy Spirit do the convicting of sin. You have no power in that department anyway. If others see Jesus in you, they will ask you questions. Then you can tell them you really have no answers, but Christ does. He has put His answers in His Word. Then you can open God's Word and learn together. You will find you have a new brother or sister in Christ. That's how you get a church off life support, leading the church to the Lifegiver one person at a time.

My little church went from not more than six people on some weeks to as many as sixty. Church became an enjoyable place to be. It isn't a social club; it's a church where members care about each other. It's a place where I can feel safe. It's a place where I strive to make others feel the same way.

It is not perfect. We haven't eliminated all our problems, but with one rule we grew week by week and year by year. We are not striving to be the biggest. We are all striving to get to heaven. Many churches say they are doing that. The difference in my opinion is we are striving together. If someone falls the only picking we want to do is pick them up, not pick them apart. Remember rule number one, and in the Spirit of Christ work together and watch your church grow.

What's Your Purpose?

Studying with a Purpose
RP1079

Sharing with a Purpose
RP1098

Praying with a Purpose
RP1155

This series focuses in on vital elements of the Christian walk: studying, sharing, and praying. Read these books to regain purpose and direction in your spiritual life and find the power that is unleashed when these elements are rightly developed!

Remnant Publications

To Order Call: (800) 423-1319
www.RemnantPublications.com

Studying With a Purpose
Lesson Series
by Author Rudy Hall
(Set of 10)

We all have questions. What better place to go than God's Word. What is my purpose for being here? Does God really have a plan for me? Does it really matter what I do? Why so many religions? This lesson series will help to answer these questions and others through a life giving study of God's word.

Remnant Publications

To Order Call: (800) 423-1319
www.RemnantPublications.com